SEDONA:
Psychic Energy Vortexes

Valley of the Sun Publishing, Box 38, Malibu, CA 90265

Dick Sutphen Presents

SEDONA:
Psychic Energy Vortexes

Edited By Dawn Abbey
From the Dick Sutphen Material

Other Metaphysical Books
By Dick Sutphen

Know Thy Higher Self
You Were Born Again To Be Together
Past Lives, Future Loves
Unseen Influences
How to Start A Successful Metaphysical Career
The Master of Life Manual
Past-Life Therapy in Action
    (with Lauren Leigh Taylor)

For complete information about
Sutphen Seminars
or for a catalog of books
and over 300 self-help and
self-exploration tapes,
write:
**Valley of the Sun
Box 38, Malibu, CA 90265**

Cover Art: "Ancients: Transmission" © 1985 by Ted Hohl.
Collage Imagery, 990 Fulton Street #302, San Francisco,
California 94117. Reprints available.

First printing: August, 1986

ISBN: 87554-049-X
Library of Congress Card Number: 86-050562

Contents

Chapter One
Introduction to the Vortexes   **7**

Chapter Two
Psychic Migration   **21**

Chapter Three
Sedona's History/Indian Legends   **29**

Chapter Four
The Sedona/Lemuria Connection   **43**

Chapter Five
"The Lost Continent of Mu"   **61**

Chapter Six
"Ley Lines Link Sedona to
All Earth's Power Spots"   **69**

Chapter Seven
Vortex Location and Warnings   **75**

Chapter Eight
Vortex Experiments   **87**

Chapter Nine
More Vortex Experiences   **105**

Chapter Ten
What Happens At A Psychic Seminar?   **141**

Chapter Eleven
A Preview?   **167**

Chapter One
Introduction To The Vortexes
By Dick Sutphen

Sedona, Arizona—a place of awesome beauty and an extraordinary energy that is felt by every person wandering through its red-rock canyons. The first time I saw Sedona, in 1969, I instantly knew this was a special place, not only because of its magnificent beauty but because of an undeniable spiritual vibration emanating throughout the area. Over the years I've become convinced, through my own experiences and the experiences of others, and through extensive research and investigation, that the psychic energy here is greater than anywhere else in the country.

The explanation for this may come from a book called **The Romeo Error** by biologist Lyall Watson. The following is a direct quote from that book:

> Navigation is bedeviled by the fact that the earth's magnetic field is riddled with local deviations and irregularities. These faults have been very carefully plotted and the most persistent of them have become quite notorious. One of these lies off the Bahama Islands (the Bermuda Triangle), another in the English county of Sussex, and a third near Prescott in Arizona.

What Watson is describing is a vortex—a positive or negative "power spot"—where a great concentration of energy emits from the earth. Positive vortexes expand and perpetuate energy; negative vortexes destroy energy.

There are many vortexes on earth, and a good analogy might be to compare them to the acupressure points on the human body. Although there are many vortexes, there are very few **major** vortex areas; Watson's quote above pinpoints the one "near Prescott" as one of those.

Prescott and Sedona are only about 30 miles apart as the crow flies (60 miles by car over the mountains). After considerable investigation, with the assistance of many psychically oriented individuals, I have concluded that it is the Sedona vortexes of which Watson writes.

It also appears that Sedona is considered one of the major vortex areas, not because of one vortex, but because of the four powerful vortexes within a few square miles of each other. In fact, there are more vortexes concentrated in Sedona than any other area on earth. This probably explains the intense psychic vibrations in the entire area.

I first wrote about Sedona in my book, **Past Lives, Future Loves,** which was published by Simon & Schuster Pocket Books in 1978. In it, I related the results of some library research that had unearthed the following information. (From *Sedona Life* magazine, "Religion of the Red Mountains," by Heather Hughes):

> Indian legend tells us that there are four places in the world designated as "power spots" and that these four are broken into two plus two—two positive and two negative, or two "light" and two "dark." It is believed that the two "positive" places in the world are Kauai, an island in Hawaii...and Sedona, both red-rock country. Sedona and Kauai, the Indians say, are vortexes of energy in which the Great Spirit gives birth to rainbows.
>
> Indians tell us that the towering crimson peaks stimulate sensitivity and that here a man realizes his true dreams and ambitions. They also say that the mountains are like a

great magnet and that people are drawn to them because it is the home of the Great Spirit. Amid red-rock country, it is said that man comes face to face with himself and the potentials of his nature.

And from my own observations and experiences, I believe this to be true. For that reason, in April of 1983, I conducted my first **Psychic Seminar** in Sedona. Because of Sedona's incredible energy and the effects which I, as well as others, had experienced here, I felt it would be the ideal place to conduct seminars in which individuals could learn to tap into and develop the psychic potentials within themselves that we all possess to one degree or another. The results were incredible! And we've been having the seminars once or twice yearly ever since.

Although Sedona was named after pioneer woman Sedona Schnebly, a **Psychic Seminar** participant noticed what may be a cosmic joke: the name Sedona spelled backwards is "anodes"—a term relating to electrical current.

Usually, as part of my **Psychic Seminars**, the participants visit one or more of the energy vortexes. Positive vortexes are charged in one of three ways:

Electric: These are "yang," charged with the male force. When you enter the vibrational field or frequency, you will become charged emotionally and physically. The energy will stimulate and elevate consciousness. It is also ideal to eliminate depression. Some people, however, consider an electrical vortex to be a strain on someone with high blood pressure or heart problems.

Magnetic: These are "yin," charged with the female force. When you enter the vibrational field or frequency, you can expect to open psychically, becoming much more perceptive, for the effects are primarily on the subconscious mind.

9

Electromagnetic: These vortexes are a combination of electrical and magnetic—or a combination of the yin-yang forces, resulting in a perfect state of balance. When you enter the vibrational field or frequency, you can expect an expansion and elevation of consciousness. This energy is ideal to stimulate past-life memories and psychic activities.

Sedona has two electric (Bell Rock and Airport Mesa), one magnetic (Courthouse Rock, also known as Cathedral Rock) and one electromagnetic (Boynton Canyon Area) vortex.

Seminar participants have reported phenomenal experiences while meditating or using self-hypnosis in these environments. The experiences range from intense spiritual visions to impressions of what took place in these canyons long ago. Many have reported direct contact with spirit entities who remain here. One of the most common reports I've received is that automatic writing is more intensely successful here than anywhere else, and even those who are new to the technique usually have impressive results. Many of the participants have reported physical healings. For most newcomers, the entire area, not to mention the vortexes themselves, generates a physical change that virtually eliminates the need for sleep.

I have in my possession hundreds and hundreds of pages of reports of the experiences people have had in the vortexes. Yet what is most convincing to me is the fact that I have personally experienced these things, as have my wife and those closest to me. As a great understatement, I can only say that my own psychic ability and spiritual experiences in the vortexes have never been surpassed anywhere else. They have included vivid visions, past-life recall, physical healing ... even the direction to raise money to establish a Sedona spiritual center came to me in the vortex.

My very first encounter with one of the vortexes took place years ago on a warm September afternoon. A woman familiar with the area took me to it and then left, warning me not to venture into the vortex itself or even to dangle my feet over the edge. She claimed a friend of hers who had done that ended up with severe blisters on the bottoms of his feet. After sitting and meditating a while, I walked to the edge of the cliff overlooking the vortex and held my hands out over it. I could actually feel a force or a pressure pushing against my palms.

With all my work and experience in metaphysics as a guide, I decided that the vortex held no danger and, being the adventurous type, I decided to ignore the woman's warning and climb down into the vortex. What followed was an amazing afternoon of meditation, past-life experiences and a feeling of recharged aliveness.

There were no adverse physical or mental effects. In fact, as an interesting side note on this day... I was one day into a case of intestinal influenza that was hitting everyone in our area at the time. Most felt the effects for four days or more. Yet, on emerging from the vortex, all signs of the flu were gone and I experienced no more of it.

I decided the woman's friend was either a true "tenderfoot" and got the blisters from hiking to the vortex, or perhaps he was experiencing some negativity within himself or some karmic manifestation brought out by the vortex energy.

Since then I have visited the vortexes numerous times with no ill effects. That is not to say that some people do not have negative or even dangerous experiences here. I will discuss things to look out for when visiting the vortexes in the chapter on "Vortex Locations and Warnings."

Most vortex experiences are transforming, spiritual and totally renewing. The following are just several of hundreds of reports I've received about extraordinary vortex experiences. In quoting these experiences here and throughout this book, I have, in most instances, named the individuals and the city and state in which they live. However, in some cases, individuals preferred either to remain anonymous or requested that I use only their initials and/or not mention where they lived.

Perhaps their reasons are similar to those expressed by **Psychic Seminar** participant **Monica Parsley** of **Virginia Beach, Virginia,** who said we could use her name, but lamented, "I have only two regrets: that the seminar is over, and that I must return home and can't tell anyone about my experiences—not even the men I date. The eastern portion of the United States is not 'enlightened.' Even those who have a tendency to 'believe' are extremely skeptical, despite the fact that we have the A.R.E. [*The Association for Research and Enlightenment, based on the Edgar Cayce readings*] here."

Contrary to Monica's personal experiences, and those of others, our research and the positive responses to our seminars and our catalog book/tape sales show there are indeed many "enlightened" individuals in the eastern United States. The problem seems to be that when a person has a unique and unusual psychic experience like those encountered by many in Sedona, they are often afraid to mention it to others for fear of being labeled "weird" or "crazy." Therefore, you may have among your friends and acquaintances many who have had similar experiences to your own, but who were afraid to mention them to you.

Part of creating your own reality is drawing to yourself the types of people with whom you can interact on an honest and forthright basis. If your dates or friends think you're weird because you have experienced psychic phenomena, maybe you're dating or associating with the wrong people. By opening yourself up, you may be surprised with similar revelations from friends and lovers.

Obviously, "telling all" in your business environment or "pushing" your metaphysical ideas on unaccepting people is not in your best interests. But you may often find that by being yourself, your life and your relationships become better and better.

Another thing I should mention here is that the people reporting these events are not professional psychics or others who make their livings in metaphysical pursuits. They are nurses, teachers, military personnel, homemakers, and business professionals of all types. They look and act just like your neighbors, friends and relatives. Being psychic is not "weird" or unusual. Everyone is psychic to some degree. Those with an interest, like those who attend seminars or study metaphysical ideas on their own, are able to expand their abilities to see, feel and experience more than what our "normal" five senses tell us.

Often, being in a place of increased energy, such as Sedona, expands that type of higher consciousness more rapidly. Many of the people who have written to me say they never considered themselves to be psychic and were often amazed at their own experiences there. Many had had unusual experiences in Sedona before ever knowing it was a psychic energy vortex area.

But because the stigma still exists, for those who would rather not have us identify them, we respect their wishes and thank them and all those mentioned in this book for allowing us to publish the fantastic results of their experiences. In fact, you may see certain individuals' names more than once, as many encountered several different types of experiences, or wrote to us after each of several Sedona visits.

Whether identified or not, the accounts are presented in the individuals' own words (whether grammatically correct or not). Some have been edited for clarity or space considerations, as some of these letters numbered twenty pages or more!

As bizarre and amazing as these incidents are, those who experienced them insist that they really happened:

"Holding a change pouch and watch, both of which belonged to my deceased father, I tried to contact him in Boynton Canyon. The battery in the watch had been dead for many months, yet I didn't replace it. I had barely begun meditation when the watch began to work. I had not set it (and still haven't) but it has been keeping correct Arizona time since then."

Monica Parsley
Virginia Beach, Virginia
[*Editor's Note: This letter was written 24 days after her vortex visit.*]

"I realized just how protected we were in the vortex. We were exploring a rather rugged area and I fell. I don't mean just losing my balance—I WAS FALLING! Mary made a grab for me but missed. I thought, 'Oh, well, what better place to die.' I was stopped at that moment by a very solid but gentle force and pushed up on my feet. At first, I thought Mary had succeeded in grabbing me, but as I was being pushed up, I turned and looked at her. She was staring in total disbelief. From my original position to my being stopped was close to a 90-degree angle. From day one until now, I have always felt very protected and peaceful in the vortex."

Nancy Hughes
Mesa, Arizona

"I knew nothing of psychic forces, vortexes and the like when I first traveled to Sedona in 1973. I was a tourist, an avid shopper and a weaver. I came down Oak Creek Canyon from Flagstaff—a thrilling drive of hairpin turns and sheer cliffs—and entered another world. Even then I felt drawn to the area. I was energized and cleansed in a way I didn't understand and I said later that Sedona had an atmosphere that couldn't be defined.

"When I returned home to New Hampshire, I wove a wall hanging of a large rock formation which I thought was representative of all the wonderful bluffs and cliffs I had seen.

"A few years later, I again traveled to Arizona and, quite naturally, to Sedona. While I was there, I photographed a large rock formation to which I felt especially attracted—one I had not seen on my previous trip. I later learned that this particular rock is called 'Bell Rock' because of its distinctive domed shape. [*Editor's Note: Bell Rock is visible to those traveling to Sedona from the south. Since this individual entered Sedona from the northern route on her first trip, it is quite possible that she never saw it.*]

"When I again returned home and had my pictures developed, I was amazed to find that the photograph of Bell Rock almost perfectly matched the wall hanging I had woven almost three years before! Even the cloud formations were similar.

"This time, when I arrived in Sedona, I climbed part way up Bell Rock to meditate. I have never felt so peaceful. I was floating and couldn't feel my body at all. I saw Indian symbols like hieroglyphics but I couldn't tune into them. I asked what message I was to carry back with me from the energies of Bell Rock and it was simply this: 'We are here. We exist.'

"On a deeper level, I think the message is that we are all part of the same consciousness, the same life force.

15

And we can be in touch with other forms of consciousness if we listen for them and follow our own inner urges, which will guide us all on our own paths of awareness.

"Before we went up to Bell Rock, I bought a crystal— roughly pyramid-shaped with blue highlights. When I finished meditating on Bell Rock, it had turned purple and is still purple to this day."

Tina Geoffrion
Auburn, New Hampshire

"After I had gotten permission to take some stones for myself and my family, I was told, 'If the rocks will increase spirituality, TAKE THE WHOLE CANYON!'"

Carolyn Kuzma
Clarkston, Michigan

[*Editor's Note: Seminar participants often want to take home a small red rock, crystals, or other memento of the vortexes. All are asked to request permission from vortex spirits before removing anything—stones, twigs, etc.—from these sacred areas. And, of course, removing desert plants or Indian artifacts of any kind is forbidden by law.*]

"I had several interesting experiences, including becoming so 'charged up' in the Airport Mesa that I was 'flying' for two days. I worked with a pendulum in all four vortexes and noticed these interesting results: In the positive vortexes (Airport Mesa and Bell Rock), the pendulum gave its usual responses, but in the negative vortex (Cathedral or Courthouse Rock), all responses were opposite in direction.

"For example, a positive response is normally, and in the positive vortexes, clockwise for me, and a negative response is back and forth from side to side. In the negative vortex, the positive response was counterclock-

16

wise and the negative response went back and forth, forward and backward. In Boynton Canyon, the balanced vortex, the pendulum seemed confused, and gave conflicting answers if asked the same question more than once. **In all vortexes, the pendulum leaned *away* from the vortex from five to ten degrees.**

"At Bell Rock, I was able to successfully use the pendulum to guide me to some crystals, which I was given permission to take home."

Patricia A. Sawyer
Derby, Kansas

"I was the woman at the seminar who came up to ask about why my palms got so hot after meditating and you told me, after asking many questions, that I was probably a natural healer. Soon after returning home, I cut myself rather badly with a large knife ... my hands were still warm each time I remembered the self-hypnosis, so I concentrated on this and the cut healed without a scar. I told my husband, a minister, about it and he merely said that there are many things God has given us that we simply don't understand.

"I began to have severe sleep problems and it turned out that my thyroid had gone hyper (called Graves Disease). Of three possible treatments, they thought burning it out with a large dose of radiation would be best. I was burned from the inside out; had a lot of pain, and then began to have terrible headaches. I finally decided that if there were to be any healing within me, I would have to get it together and help myself. These headaches would wake me bolt upright and my throat would hurt so that I wanted to tear it out of my neck. So I prayed as the attack progressed that, if it were true that God had given me the power to heal, that it would be available to use on myself then. My hands got very hot. I laid them over my throat where the pain was, and the pain stopped dead.

"I was to go and have my blood tested the next day, for they are waiting for the thyroid to die from the radioactivity so they can begin a regimen of synthyroid. They have tested me twice so far and the thyroid is functioning normally. With the overdose they gave me and the severity of the burn, it should be dead...somehow it is functioning like a normal thyroid now. Strange?!

"You have my permission to use any or all of this letter, however, in order not to hurt or cause distress to those of my household or church, I request that you not use my name; initials are probably okay. Thank you again for all that I learned from you and the new insights that are mine."

C.D.

"I was at the Airport Vortex. A ring I was wearing on my left hand began to vibrate, and I felt great energy in the hand. I was not in trance, just relaxed, not deep. I had my eyes open. I brought my watercolors with me and did a painting. It was the first time I had done anything creative in a long time. I was told I should use my middle name to sign on my painting. This has always been a question in the back of my mind, as my first name is rather plain, but I felt that my middle name is too pretentious. It was an extremely emotional experience. I'm sure I will never be the same. I had the feeling that it was telling me to be myself and not be so serious."

Mabel Brazillia Fischer
Panguitch, Utah

"At Boynton Canyon, I meditated in hopes of having a psychic, higher-consciousness experience with my husband, who died two-and-a-half years ago. I believe that connection was made and we were able to have a final, inclusive, closing conversation. This was very satisfying to me, as he had died instantly in a car accident. I found myself discussing all the significant moments of our marriage and how I have grown and developed in ways I wouldn't have imagined. All the anger over the 'how could you just walk out the door and never come back— you've got a lot of nerve' melted away finally. The 'conversation' was the best of me and the best of him and I believe we let our relationship go free this time around with love and understanding and a great deal of appreciation for each other that we were able to do it. I will never forget Boynton Canyon."

Mary Hinckley
Portland, Oregon

"It's easier to 'open' in an accepting, feeling environment. At Sedona, during the playing of the 'Jonathan Livingston Seagull" theme, I understood in a flash the why and how of two experiences with two different persons in this life that balanced my karma. On Bell Rock, the capricious spirit whom I love, who had chosen to hang himself three years ago on this day, made sure I knew that he had really arrived. He jabbed me in the ribs and brought me to my feet—flat out of meditation. We know I don't convince casually! One reason I am here is to accept what I know—that I had to NOT stop him from doing what he did."

Leah Johnson
Rockledge, Florida

Chapter Two
Psychic Migration

Upon first arriving in Sedona, you cannot help but perceive a subtle but powerful force. The vortex energy expands and intensifies your own energy and the energy generated between people. If the existing energy is primarily positive, it increases the positive quality. The reverse is also true: the vortex energy will intensify negativity, which can be undesirable.

Because of these intense vibrations, when couples move to Sedona, their relationship either becomes far better than it was previously, or the intensity pulls them apart and the relationship ends. I feel the local energy expands and intensifies the existing energy between two people. If their energy is primarily positive, it increases the positive quality of their shared life. But if their relationship contains negative aspects, the local energy can be expected to intensify the negativity as well, which can cause problems. I've always felt it's a subconscious karmic decision when a couple decides to relocate here.

And many do so as a result of spontaneously arrived at decisions:

"I first came to Sedona to attend Dick's May 1984 **Psychic Seminar**. When not at the seminar, all I could do was cry and say, 'I am HOME!' I called home to Riverside, California, and told my husband, Larry, 'We are moving!' We arrived in Sedona to live in April 1985. Home AT LAST!"

Randi Mabrey
Sedona, Arizona

"My husband and I were ready for a change. We were living in Princeton, New Jersey, and felt an urge to move west. I was researching the Anazazi Indians and wanted to find a central location where I could do my work. We remembered driving through Sedona once very quickly on our way somewhere else and remembered we liked the town, but we couldn't remember anything about it. Can you imagine? We didn't 'remember' the red rocks or anything! But right then we decided to move there anyway and we've lived here happily now for three years."

Kathie Dame-Glerum
Sedona, Arizona

"As soon as we began driving down from the airport, I had the feeling of coming home. I seemed to know where everything was, although I have never been to Sedona before ... plus a very calm, peaceful feeling, a feeling of finally belonging. At the Boynton Canyon vortex, I did a short meditation and asked whether I should move to Arizona, as I have been planning to do so for about two years. My answer, upon coming out of meditation, was a cloud in the shape of an Indian arrowhead, pointing directly at the large monolith-like rock. I took this to be a very visually affirmative answer."

Patricia Adkiss
Council Bluffs, Iowa

"I found, upon leaving Sedona, a feeling of leaving home. This was my first visit, but the place captured my heart and I know I will be returning to Sedona regularly."

Name Withheld
Long Beach, California

"As soon as we entered Sedona, I spoke to the real estate agent about property values in Sedona. I promised to get back to him, but I never got the opportunity to do so.

"My friends and I stayed over one more day in Sedona after the **Psychic Seminar** so that we could explore the vortexes at our leisure. We went to Bell Rock and I climbed to a comfortable level and settled down to say my rosary. I have been troubled and uncertain for many months now. My husband is paralyzed on his right side with a stroke, and other personal factors in my life have left me feeling as though I am in limbo. Upon completing my prayers, I put my head down on my knees and prayed that I be shown the way; that I receive confirmation of things to come; that I was on the right path, and that I be given a sign.

"Suddenly, I began slowly rocking from side to side, the tears streamed uncontrollably down my face and the rocking became stronger and stronger. As it increased in intensity, I became very frightened and called to my friends. They came and placed their hands on my shoulders and, gradually, the rocking stopped.

"After leaving the vortex, we made our way back to the real estate agent. He showed me a home in the Chapel Development, directly below the Chapel of the Holy Cross and in clear view of Bell Rock, where I received my inspiration. I gave him a down payment and purchased the home. I certainly had been given a sign. It was an experience I shall never forget. I know I was guided there."

**Kitty Kelly
Stanton, California**

Lots of people have been heeding the call to move West since the early '70s. I wrote about this phenomenon in my book, **Past Lives, Future Loves.** It continues to be true even now.

For many years, Arizona has been the leading psychic center in the country. The psychic concentration is within a one-hundred-mile circle that includes Phoenix/Scottsdale, Sedona and Prescott. The Phoenix/Scottsdale metropolitan area, of course, is well-known. Prescott is a typical old Arizona cowboy town situated in a mountain valley and surrounded by a national forest preserve. Like Sedona, it is rapidly becoming a haven for those wishing to escape the stress of big-city life.

People from everywhere have been, and are being, directed to relocate in the Prescott/Sedona area and they have moved their entire families thousands of miles because they felt it was important. Also, psychic practitioners, writers and those dedicated to philosophy come in increasing numbers.

Whenever I ask newcomers 'why?' the answer is always, "We were told to come." There are many psychic migration theories and none of them negates the others, so all could be valid. Most have to do with "energy." In the Bradshaw Mountain area, some say it is the mountaintop elevation and the pine trees. Pine trees are supposed to provide more life energy to the atmosphere than any other plant or tree. It is a somewhat generally accepted belief that if you stand on the north side of a pine tree and hug it, you will be "recharged." I don't know if I accept that or not, but it is an interesting idea and I've been known to hug a few myself.

In Los Angeles, an old Sioux Indian woman—a shaman who had once worked with Black Elk—told me, "I've had a great vision and in it Chief Gall came to me and told me to go to Arizona. It was here that the movement would form and spread. An Indian symbol would guide the way."

Many feel that something is supposed to happen here or from here. Sedona is supposedly situated over an ancient Lemurian city and many have experienced impressions of confirmation of this concept.

There is something about the energy source of the entire area that no one really understands. Phoenix has always been known as "the valley of healing," even by the original Indians who settled there. A "special" energy is again given as the reason. There are hundreds of metaphysically oriented churches and organizations in the Phoenix metropolitan area.

Another concept is that all great religions or spiritual philosophies have been launched from desert areas. Supposedly, desert energy is conducive to evolutionary thinking. Prescott and Sedona are surrounded by high desert and Phoenix/Scottsdale are Sonoran desert.

Maybe it is "energy" that is pulling people together. Past-life soul grouping energy, some cosmic energy as in the Sedona vortexes, or the mental energies of like-minded people. It doesn't matter how, only that there is evident momentum.

If these things are happening by "plan," then I feel it is your plan and only through your own acceptance will changes occur. You will certainly never be forced to develop psychic abilities, or find out about your past lives and associations, or to relocate to a metaphysical geographic location. You control and create your own reality in these things as in all others.

Of all the areas of the Southwest, Arizona seems to be the most mystical, the most spiritual and contains some of the most beautiful areas known anywhere in the world. Even the origin of the name, Arizona, is a mystery. Cynics might tell you it stands for "arid zone."

However, in 1877, journalist Hiram C. Hodge published a book about his travels in Arizona from 1874-76.

In his book, reprinted in 1962 under the title **1877 Arizona As It Was,** Hodge related what he claims was an Aztec legend that explains the origin of the name:

Of the origin and significance of the name, Arizona, there seems to be much doubt, and a score or more of definitions have been given by different and well-informed persons. Referring back to the old Aztec traditions, the following significant item occurs, which may assist somewhat in the explanation:

"The earth is the offspring of the sky. Long prior to the present race of men, the earth was peopled by a race of giants who in time died off, leaving the earth uninhabited. After a long time, a celestial virgin, a child of one of the thirteen deities who rule all things, came down to the earth, and being well pleased, remained for a long time its sole inhabitant. Once when in a deep sleep, a drop of dew from heaven fell on her, and she conceived and bore two children, a son and daughter, from whom have sprung all the people of the earth. The name of this celestial virgin was Arizunna, the beautiful, or sun beloved maiden." The Mohave language, which is by far the most perfect and complete of any of the Indian dialects of the country, has two words of nearly the same meaning: Ari, meaning the sun, holy, good, or beautiful; and Urnia, maid or maiden; which together means the land of the beautiful or lovely maiden. This may be the true meaning of the word Arizona. Another definition is this, Ari, from the Mohave, meaning beautiful or good, and Zona, from the Spanish, a zone, and taken together, meaning the land of the beautiful zone. Both of these definitions are well made, and are quite significant and expressive.

It is well-established fact that in the time when Hodge was writing about Arizona, the white man was abysmally ignorant of the Indian tribes of the area. Therefore, we cannot be sure this legend is indeed from the Aztec. Referring to his mention of perfection of the Mohave language, it is interesting to note that the Mohave are one of many tribes that speak a language that is related to the language of the Yavapai. These languages are known as Yuman langauges. Also, the Yavapai were often mistakenly called "Mohave-Apache." Even today, the government agency in charge of setting up the reservation named it Fort McDowell Mohave-Apache Reservation, even though they are Yavapai.

The Mohave referred to the Yavapai as the "People of the Sun" (enyaeva—sun; pai—the people). This information becomes increasingly interesting when compared to the Indian legends surrounding Sedona, which we will relate in the next chapter.

Chapter Three
Sedona's History/Indian Legends

Sedona is located 120 miles north of Phoenix in the central Arizona mountains at a 4,300-foot elevation. The area is known as "red-rock country" because the magnificent red-rock formations are unique in the state and cover only a few square miles. Sedona's beautiful terrain is often featured in national publications and as the background in many television commercials. More than 75 major motion pictures have been filmed there, especially the big-budget, epic Westerns.

Modern Sedona is an art colony with outstanding galleries and is the home of many well-known artists and writers. The village of Tlaquepaque has become world-famous as an architectural showpiece of Spanish Colonial design. It houses major galleries and shops and is a highlight to the millions of annual visitors.

Sedona was founded June 26, 1902, when the post office was established. According to Albert E. Thompson in "The Story of Sedona," from the book **Those Early Days ...**—a collection of old-timers' memoirs published by the Sedona Westerners—before 1902 the place was known as Camp Garden. It was named Sedona after the Post Office Department rejected the name Schnebly Station as being too long for postmarks. Sedona Schnebly and her husband, Theodore C. Schnebly, had settled there a year before. Schnebly became the first postmaster.

But where did Sedona Schnebly get her unusual name? According to her son, Ellsworth M. Schnebly, who wrote "How Sedona Was Named" in **Those Early Days...**, it was a product of her mother's inspiration·

Numerous uninformed, and perhaps, well-intentioned people have speculated on how Sedona got its name and what the name means. Sedona is not an Indian nor a Mexican name. One omnipotent individual explained it this way: When T. C. was courting Sedona, he said, 'This week end I am going over to see Dona." [*Editor's Note: According to this same account, Sedona became known affectionately by her neighbors as "Aunt Dona."*]

My mother's parents were Pennsylvania Dutch and did not even know any Mexicans or Indians back there. ... they reared twelve children including my mother. Grandmother said that she did not know why, but that she liked Sedona as a name and gave it to my mother. She had never heard of the name and after all, there is a first time that any word or name is used.

The Indians hold the Sedona red-rock area as sacred. Legends passed down through generations tell of an Indian goddess with supernatural powers who lived here and passed the ancient knowledge to the Yavapais through her grandson, The First Man.

Before she died in 1966 at the age of 88, Yavapai Chieftess Viola Jimulla related her remembrance of the legend to Franklin Barnett, who published it in his biography of her, **Viola Jimulla: The Indian Chieftess:**

The legend about the creation of the Yavapai Indians is based upon the belief that there were, or are, four different cycles or worlds.

30

The first people emerged from underground and were terminated by the flood; the second was the time of the Goddess Komwida Pokwee (Old Woman Rock) and her grandson Skata-amcha (Skadkama); the third ended by world fire; and we are living in the fourth today. The story is that they, the Yavapais, came from underground and that they climbed through a large hole made by a huge pine tree with vines hanging from the tree into the hole. They used the vine to pull themselves to the surface of the earth.

"Komwida Pokwee, as a girl came from the flood (first cycle of Yavapai creation) and settled in the Red Rock country near what is now Sedona. She came when the earth was still wet (second cycle of creation). Komwida Pokwee is the Goddess of the supernatural and medicine powers, and is beautiful and as pure as a downy white feather. Skataamcha is her grandson and all of the songs, supernatural powers, and medicine power and knowledge were given to him by his grandmother, and were passed on to the Yavapai medicine men and their people. The medicine men, or anyone believing in the religion, may see her yet in a vision or dream and receive instructions, comfort and encouragement. These two, together, Komwida Pokwee and Skataamcha, always set a good exmaple for our Yavapai people to follow."

Unfortunately, like the Yavapai people themselves, these legends have become scattered and lost. Comparison of Viola's version to the following, that of Mike Harrison, born in 1886, oldest man of the Fort McDowell

31

Yavapai community, and John Williams, born 1904, showed similar concepts but different details. Notice in particular the spelling of the names. These could possibly be phonetic or just mistranslations.

This account was taken from the book, **The Yavapai of Fort McDowell** by Sigrid Khera:

> We come out at Sedona, the middle of the world. This is our home. ... We call Sedona Wipuk. We call it after the rocks in the mountains there. Some of my people, they call themselves Wipukpa. That's the ones who live up there around Sedona. All Yavapai come from Sedona. But in time they spread out.

> North of Camp Verde there is Montezuma Well. We call it Ahagaskiaywa. The lake has no bottom and underneath the water spreads out wide. That's where the people come out first.

> ... That first chief from down the Well, we see him on the sky early in the morning. He is up there, the morning star. ... Lots of people come up from there, quail, rabbits, jackrabbits. And at the time when they are up, they all speak Yavapai. They get up on top and when they look back the water is coming. ... The flood is in the Well. But the water doesn't come out. Just stays level in there.

> ... After some time there comes another flood. The people put a girl in a hollow log. Put food in that log for her. The woodpecker made a small hole for her in the log. Then they tell her: "The flood will raise you. You will hit the sky. But just lay still. If you lay still, you will get out in the end." Then the people glued the log together with pitch, with ahpihl.

The girl lay still in there all the time. After some time the water went down. The girl had a dove with her and she sent that dove out. She sent her out and the dove come back with a little seed. So the water was gone. There at Sedona there is a high place. It is the highest place all around. And when the water went down, the log hit that high place. It stopped right there. And the girl came out from the log.

We call that girl Kamalapukwia. That means "Old Lady White Stone." She had a white stone. And that white stone is the one which protects the women. Her name means she got that kind of stone. She is the first woman on earth and she got that stone. She is the first woman and we come from her. She came out at Sedona and that's where all Indians come from.

Kamalapukwia lived in a cave in Sedona. Kamalapukwia was all alone. One morning she ran over to Mingus Mountain. Lay down there before the sun came up. The sun comes up and hits her inside. After that she went to that Cave where the water drips down all the time. She lay down and the water came down and hit her. Made her a baby. A little girl.

When that girl came to age, Kamalapukwia said to her, "Daughter, they did that and you come up. You go over there and do like I did. So we have another people." They were the only two people. So they were lonely and wanted another human. The girl said, "All right." ... She got pregnant and then got the little baby, it was a boy: Sakarakaamche.

When that boy was still a baby, a bald eagle killed his mother. ... Now there were only two

33

people: the old lady Kamalapukwia and the little boy Sakarkaamche. The old lady raised the little boy.

...The old lady, she told Sakarakaamche everything. Teach him everything. And he learned from his father, the Cloud. Sakarakaamche knew everything about the weeds which cure all sicknesses (from his grandmother). We don't know where she learned it, but Sakarakaamche learned it from her. And he is the one who is teaching the humans who come up.

...He gave us four sacred things: he gave us the Blackroot, the yellow powder, the blue stone and the white stone.

Blackroot is a very great medicine. We call it isamaganyach. It helps against pains and sores. It makes you feel good again.

The yellow powder, we call it achitawsa. It is the pollen from the cattail. The medicine man, when he heals somebody, he puts yellow powder on him. Yellow powder stands for the light. It helps you think and talk right.

The blue stone and white stone, that's what protects us from bad things. The blue stone stands for men, the white stone for the women. When you have these stones and think well, bad things can't hit you. The blue stone that people wear on a ring, that's not the one that protects them. It is like a toy. But when it is blessed by a medicine man, then it will help.

We can't be certain, but from the story of the Yavapai men, we would assume that the blue stone and the white stone they are referring to are turquoise, so prominent in jewelry of all Southwestern Indian tribes, and white

34

quartz crystal, which is found embedded in the red rocks of Sedona.

One thing that has always interested me is the number of people who, after experiencing the vortexes at Sedona, relate having experiences with Indian spirits. These experiences seem to correlate with these very obscure Indian legends, of which I have not previously written or talked about to seminar participants. The extent of our knowledge before researching this book was the story we had heard that Boynton Canyon near Sedona was home of the "Great Mother."

These legends are not widely known, even in local areas, as little is written about the Yavapai. Because in the late 1800s, white soldiers moved the Yavapai to many different areas in Arizona, they were often mistaken for members of other tribes. They were even thought to be a branch of the Apache tribe, to which they are not at all related, even by language. We had to do quite a bit of searching in local Arizona libraries to find these somewhat rare books about the Yavapai.

Even though we are, for the first time, publishing anything about these Indian legends, it is amazing that experiences of participants of past Sedona **Psychic Seminars** relate specific details that correspond to these ancient tales.

For instance, many claim to see Indian spirits or guides, a not too unlikely situation since, being in the West, one might relate his or her experiences to Western concepts of "cowboys and Indians." However, rarely does anyone ever claim to see pioneers, covered wagons, cowboys or gold miners, all of which were also very prevalent in the area—only Indians.

In fact, I have had only **two** reports regarding such experiences in Sedona seminars—one from a man who says he saw himself as a cowboy in a past life who was rejected by his contemporaries because he defended the plight of the Indians. He eventually went to live with his Indian brothers.

A woman who experienced being a pioneer woman in a past life gave this account: "While in meditation, listening to the joyous laughter of the children on your 'sounds' tape and viewing a scene of me in an early settler's home on the prairie, for some unexplained reason, the laughter made me, a pioneer woman, want to cry. What had happened back then?"

Many possibilities, either from a present life situation or a past life, may have triggered this woman's tears. It is known that empathetic individuals often are able to pick up the vibrations of past events in an area. With this in mind, it is interesting to note that the pioneer woman for whom Sedona was named, suffered a tragedy with one of her children. Because of it, she had to leave the area and spent several years in emotional recovery before returning to Sedona.

Ellsworth M. Schnebly, son of Sedona, relates this tragic tale in **Those Early Days...**:

> Pearl and I each had a gentle pony on which we rode all around the area, happily and fearlessly, until June 12th, 1905, when Pearl was dragged to death by her pony. Mother, Baby Sister (Genevieve), Pearl and I were driving the cattle home from the unfenced range that evening when one cow darted from the herd. Pearl's trained pony instinctively started after the cow, throwing Pearl and scaring itself. The pony raced across Oak Creek, dragging the lifeless, mangled body to the corral gate where we found it when we caught up. Mother had been in excellent health but this tragedy upset her tremendously

and she began to weaken from grief and worry. Not long after, the doctor advised Dad to sell and move away or risk losing his wife. Seemingly there was no alternative, so they sold the place to my Uncle Ellsworth and returned to Gorin, Missouri.

...in 1929, they returned to the beautiful red rock area where they had become deep-rooted long ago to join their pioneering neighbors and the community that bore the name of my mother.

Was this woman tuning in to the death of Sedona Schnebly's daughter? Who knows?

However, because of the sacredness of this area to the Indians, it seems that most of the vibrations picked up by those in Sedona have to do with Indians.

Another statement from the two Yavapai men might explain why this is, and why it may not be just participants' imaginations. The Indians believe that spirits that look like Indians do inhabit the sacred places, especially the mountainous areas. They even claim that under certain conditions, these spirits are visible:

...The Kakaka are just like Indians, but little people. Maybe three or four feet high. They live in the mountains, Four Peak, Red Mountain, Superstition, Granite Mountain near Prescott. They can get in and out the mountain. They are just like the wind, like air. You can hear them hollering at night and sometimes some people can see them. The Kakaka never die. They were around this country before the people. ... They keep watching over us all the time.

37

Others experience the visitation of an Indian woman or women and, I suppose, because we have talked about the concept of the "Great Mother," some may relate what they see to that idea. But there are a greater than average number of visions and experiences that relate directly to the story of the Goddess and her daughter. Even the details of many individuals' experiences seem similar. Also, notice how birds play a role in the perceptions. Remember that the Goddess sent a dove out of the log ... an eagle ate the mother of The First Man. The color white is also prevalent. Chieftess Viola described the Goddess as "beautiful and pure as a downy white feather."

These are some of the experiences related by seminar participants:

"Sitting on a ledge looking over Boynton Canyon in meditation, I saw an old Indian woman and then a young, beautiful Indian maiden."

Jeanne Arnew
Prescott, Arizona

"At Airport Mesa, I had a strong feeling of peace and perceived a gentle female presence. I then saw the Great Mother weep. She is very tall, slender and wears a white dress. Her hair is long, blows in the wind and the crows play in her hair. The sparrow and the eagle became symbols of the Great Mother."

Pat Cambell
Pacifica, California

"We visited Boynton Canyon and found a spot in the dry creek bed where we laid our crystals out to charge them in the sun. Right before we decided to leave, I felt a shaking of my soul as I perceived a huge Indian woman rise up from the center of the canyon. She stood about 200 feet tall and was dressed in white buckskin. She was beautiful. I just sat there in awe. She looked at me and smiled, then turned slowly, motioning to all of the area as if to say, 'This is my land. I am guardian here.' She smiled and slowly was enveloped by the canyon floor once again. It wasn't until we returned to the seminar that Dick explained about the Great Mother. I know I saw her."

Randi Mabrey
Sedona, Arizona

"Cathedral Rock: A smiling young woman dressed in white—apparently mestizo (Spanish/Indian mix). 'The serious search for spiritual development must be balanced with joy and happiness—and will be.' Her name: Neena (Nina?)."

Frank H. Small III
Gaithersburg, Maryland

"At Cathedral, or Courthouse, Rock, one of the resident birds swooped at me and yelled just as I was calling the vortex spirit. As we were leaving, I was given a feather from the wing tip of a eagle. This has a special significance, since the name of the vortex spirit who worked with me and whom I have a past-life tie is Eagle Feather. Also, in that past life, I was a leader and medicine man of the Eagle Clan."

Patricia A. Sawyer
Derby, Kansas

"I did have a very brief flash of two images. One was that of an Indian Eagle God (I don't even know if such a god exists in mythology). He was suspended with arms spread out, in front of the cliffs across the valley, and had eagle feathers on his arms and body. The second image

was right behind the Eagle God and was of cliff
dwellings."

R. H. W.
Woodland Hills, California

"With my eyes open, I studied the face of the rock
formations, seeing the faces of Indians and animals."

E. Kay Hood
Birmingham, Michigan

"Boynton Canyon ... I became very aware of Indian
presence ... peaceful and loving, but that it was their
'ground' and we were visitors to absorb and learn from
the vibrations offered for the advancement and pro-
gression of humankind."

Sandy Tofflemire
Lawndale, California

As Yavapai Chieftess Viola Jimulla stated, "...anyone
believing in the religion, may see her [*the Goddess*] yet in
a vision or dream and receive instructions, comfort and
encouragement."

Recall that the Yavapai men said, "That first chief
from down the Well, we see him on the sky early in the
morning. He is up there, the morning star."

Although she seems to be referring to a woman, relate
these details to what **A. Jean Jensen** of **Pleasanton,
California,** wrote:

"We hiked into Boynton Canyon. After going into
trance, I did some automatic writing. Here is what I
wrote: 1058, a village of Pueblo-type Indians lived here ...
in area 2,500 years. There was a great flood in the
canyon, many people died. I was saved. Morning Star is
my name. You saw me dancing in your dream last night.
I am one of your guides. My one son became Chief

40

Towatchapee when his father died. My son died young in a battle with other Indians, there was much grief and wailing. My father was the tribal medicine man. After the flood, we moved to the village where Sedona is now. I lived to be 60 years of age."

"On Saturday, after the vortex orientation, my companions and I headed for Boynton Canyon. From what we had heard and read, this seemed to be the place for us. While driving, when we were about two miles from the vortex, someone remarked that they were feeling very calm and peaceful. The words that suddenly came out of my mouth were: "I don't. I feel like laughing." And that is exactly what I did! I laughed, and the laughter grew until my sides hurt and tears were streaming down my face. I had difficulty catching my breath enough to stop. I felt as if I had been laughing a very long time, although the incident only lasted a few seconds. When the laughter stopped, the ache in my side went away.

"The laugh was not my laugh ... it sounded like a young woman. Since I am not known for uncontrollable emotions, including laughter—my own being far more raucous when it can be heard, with the sound frequently catching in my throat—I knew that this was not my laughter. This was totally different: joyous, uninhibited, youthful, playful ... almost tingling.

"As we were hiking out, talking and sharing vortex experiences after having spent several hours in the vortex, the uncontrollable laughter began again. I tried to pay attention to the sound and how I felt, but I was overcome with all the joyful laughter.

"I shared the information at the evening session and afterwards was told by two women who are doing research on the area, that they too had a similar

41

experience. They said their giggles lasted for most of a weekend. They told me that, so far, they had only discovered one female spirit in the area; her name is Running Deer.

"A week before the seminar, I had a dream about Indians, which is odd because I could not recall having dreamed about Indians before. The Indian woman in the dream was named 'Running Deer.'"

Delores Saint

"It took some time for me to relax and go into a meditation. Then my guide came and took me to join Indians and I danced with them in their 'Friendship Dance.' I was given permission to take three small stones: one for my husband, who has emphysema, one for me to use at home, and a tiny one to put in my billfold. I know the Spirits are in the stones. When I hold them in my hand, I feel so calm, warm and loving."

Polly Carter

Chapter Four
The Sedona/Lemuria Connection

Another interesting correlation I have found in the experiences of seminar participants is the number of people who seem to tap into the idea that an ancient city existed (some say it still exists underground) in the area that is now Sedona. Many people have related visions of energy fields generated by crystals, advanced civilizations or extraterrestrial beings, and some kind of cataclysmic event—most often a terrible flood. We have read in preceding chapters how the Indian legends describe great floods and god-like beings who escaped the destruction. Does it all relate?

Since I first began spending time in Sedona, I've had metaphysically oriented people tell me that there is an ancient Lemurian city buried beneath the great red-rock formations and canyons that now comprise the terrain, or that Sedona somehow relates to Lemuria. Close friends, whom I respect for their psychic abilities, have related visions of unusual, ancient structures that appear in various areas. Some have seen visions of these structures in the sky above Sedona.

In re-examining regressions I have conducted with individuals over the years and comparing them with the trance communications of Edgar Cayce, Ruth Montgomery and Lemuria's primary historian, Colonel James Churchward, I find general agreement about many facts regarding Lemurian history.

According to Churchward, Lemuria was a huge Pacific continent unconnected to what is now the North American continent. He relates four great cataclysms;

the third, and worst, transpired 80,000 years ago. The final cataclysm took place 12,000 years ago, and sent Mu and millions of her inhabitants to the depths of the sea in a "vortex of fire and water."

This seems to relate quite closely with the Edgar Cayce trance readings. Both agree that the Lemurians had ample warning of the impending catastrophe; for centuries, people left the motherland to establish colonies in areas such as Egypt, Peru, Central America and Mexico.

All the metaphysical writers and researchers seem to agree that the Lemurians were a spiritual, peaceful people. They developed a very just and fair governmental system; one of their great rulers was a woman. The populace was composed of highly skilled artisans and craftsmen. They enjoyed a very advanced form of civilization, with great cities and impressive temples, and many Lemurians attained a Universal perspective.

There is little scientific argument that a great land mass once existed above water in the Pacific, where only Lemurian mountain tops remain today as islands. In the Mexican temple of Uxmal, an inscription declares that the structure was dedicated to the memory of Mu, "the lands to the west, that land of Kui, the birthplace of our sacred mysteries." The temple faces west, the direction of the lost continent.

In her book, **The World Before**, Ruth Montgomery, through automatic writing controlled by her guides, relates that the huge heads on Easter Island in the Pacific mark the site of a great Lemurian ceremonial center.

In Edgar Cayce's reading #812-1, the "sleeping prophet" talked about a woman named 'A-mel-elia," a priestess in the "Temple of Light," who was an overseer of communications between various lands. The reading mentions Mu and a "particular portion of Arizona and Nevada that are as a portion of the Brotherhood of those people from Mu."

According to Churchward, Lemuria was known as the "Land of the Sun" and "Empire of the Sun." In his book, **The Sacred Symbols of Mu**, Churchward also claims that the cliff-dwelling Indians of Arizona and New Mexico were once residents of Lemuria. The cliff dwellings of Montezuma's Castle are now maintained for public visitation by the U.S. Park Service ... and they are only a few miles from Sedona.

The Hopi Indian reservation and mesas are also very close to Sedona. Hopi legend claims that the tribe came to their current area from the West after their world was destroyed. They traveled on bamboo rafts until coming to a wall of steep mountains which they climbed; as they looked back, they could see islands sinking behind them.

Another interesting fact, that may or may not relate to Lemuria, was pointed out to me by author/scientist Dr. Patrick Flanagan. Pat was studying United States air pollution maps attained via satellite. Only two places in this country indicated perfectly clear air: a tiny spot around the top of Mount Shasta in California, and the area around Sedona, Arizona.

Sedona is higher than Phoenix and lower than nearby Prescott, so why should this be? Possible explanations could be in the intense energy emitting from the vortexes in Sedona or, as the Indians believe, the area is a sacred, spiritual ground and is thus protected. And ... maybe, as several of my seminar participants perceived, there is a great Lemurian crystal buried beneath Sedona that is emitting the intense energy.

During the May 1984 **Psychic Seminar**, which I conducted with psychic Alan Vaughan, I decided to run an experiment. After little prior discussion, I hypnotized the participants and asked them to perceive any information they could attain regarding the Sedona/Lemuria connection. I left it open as to how they would attain the knowledge: ESP, remote viewing, general regressions, or simply tapping into the collective unconscious.

When the session was complete, we discussed the results as a group and attained a general consensus about the connection. I asked those who were willing to share their experiences to write them down. A distillation of their individual communications reveals that 23 people received the "essence" of ancient, highly evolved people who relate to Lemuria.

Seven sensed that a large crystal lies buried somewhere beneath the red earth of the area. Several felt that the name Lemuria was incorrect.

Here, in their own words, are the experiences of some of the participants:

"People of Mu colonized in the Sedona area after the great disaster of the motherland. Their original colony here was leveled by a glacier which carved the canyons and is now beneath the earth. A large crystal is beneath this area. It is a geometric shape with another crystal inside. The crystal is the real source of the vortex power."

Tiena-Kay Halm
Glendale, California

"There is an ancient city beneath Sedona, but Lemuria does not sound right to me. There is a crystal temple here, as in Atlantis, hence the energy vortex. It is my feeling that souls are congregating together in places like Sedona. It's like a reward for a 'good incarnation': after a few lives, the reward is getting to come back to your source. Sounds far-fetched, right? But there is a definite purpose and plan for this. Sedona is a place of departure and arrival; it feels like an airport terminal. The energy is of such a high vibration that it attracts those travelling on different planes and dimensions, as well as those already here. So there are different dimensional souls now merging with the souls that have been here a long time. Each is exploring and learning from the others. It is very exciting, intellectual, learning and sharing. Like a conference of all the Nobel Prize winners."

Sharon L. Petek
Pueblo, Colorado

"The name Lemuria is incorrect. I think it might be a 'chanted' sound, something like 'La-Mu.' I visualized a giant monolith expressing tremendous energy. It is time to establish the latent powers within; that is why we have returned to our former home for reunion and re-creation."

Vicki Heller
Long Beach, New York

"A large crystal is buried beneath Sedona. Where Sedona is now, there was a city before ... and it still exists! The name was not Lemuria; was destroyed by another power, but not completely. The city still exists, but on a different frequency."

Marianne Brijer
Renton, Washington

"There is a crystal in Boynton Canyon where the land folds into itself; solstices, equinoxes and planetary alignments give energy to the other vortexes. There is great rejuvenation here as there has always been.

"I perceived a 'Temple of Learning' or 'Temple of Healing.' I don't get a sense of any buildings at all. The lifeforms of high light and high vibration didn't seem to need any. The Tenders of the Crystal, who were lower in vibration and lesser evolved, needed the shelter, however, and lived in the caves surrounding the area. The highly evolved forms transmitted knowledge wordlessly, through the use of the crystal.

"The Tenders of the caves were not people to emulate. Knowledge of them will not serve any purpose; they were animalistic, keepers only, and not of the Knowledge. When the crystal was destroyed (covered?) during the earth changes, many of the Knowledgeable Ones chose simply to leave their bodies so that they could return to teach when the crystal was again found. And it was the ignorance of the unknowledgeable ones that kept the crystal hidden after the earth changes—hidden from those who would destroy it as well as those who would harness the power.

"In an altered state, I can picture the crystal quite clearly as a large, disc-shaped convex. It is now lying upside down.

"P.S.: I have a sense that great power could be had by charging a large crystal, placed in a circle of stones— each one gathered from the other vortex areas and laid in the sun—above the main crystal in Boynton Canyon."

Kathie Dame-Glerum
Sedona, Arizona

"I didn't have any experiences at the vortex on my first trip Saturday afternoon, but I sure could feel the power. Saturday night, in the regression, was a different story.

"I perceived that I was working on the support structure for a crystal. I knew that this was to throw a beam of energy, somthing like a laser beam. I headed a group that was devising a crystal to expand the power of the 'great crystal' to the farthest reaches of the earth.

48

And I knew that there were people who worked at the 'great crystal' who were not happy with me for doing this because they were going to lose some control.

"When I responded to your next suggestion, Dick, I saw myself in a balloon basket—that doesn't seem to make sense, but I was looking down into a valley, and it seemed to be in this area, in the Sedona area. And there were two high gate posts with a gate going through it; beyond that, a huge concrete slab, or something flat, like a landing area. And to the right were the buildings where we were working on the crystal.

"I know that was here because the vortex was here. I also know that we were meeting with highly evolved beings who were giving us the plans on how to build this 'sending station.'

"My next impression was of a great explosion, and I knew the great crystal had been destroyed. I think some people attempted to manipulate the energy in an attempt to destroy us, but it must have backfired or something. I don't understand it; the experience has left me very shaken."

Name Withheld
Phoenix, Arizona

"I perceived a buried large crystal or, maybe, a special stone. It was creating a form of powerful energy, like a buried transmitter, in the Boynton Canyon area. My most intense impressions were of the great sense of love and harmony in this area."

Charlotte Reeves
Fremont, California

"In the Lemurian regression, I was an old man with long, white hair and beard, shiny metallic dress and shoes. And I was in what appeared to be a cave-like room ablaze with light. The light came from crystals arranged in a pentagram. People would come to me, down escalator-like stairs, to be healed—or rather, to stay well. They would sit in the pentagram; it was as if everyone came to do this. It was just a part of the lifestyle and was necessary in order to stay well.

"The Sedona area was a healing center, and the healing was always conducted in the cave, which was definitely below the ground, deep in the earth. I was really impressed by the brightness of the crystals in the cave."

Marlys Cates
Del Mar, California

"My guide took me to a cave that he said was the entrance to the Inner City. It is in Boynton Canyon. The cave was dark, but crystals lit the way. The deeper we went into the cave, the lighter it became. We came around a curve, and the crystals were so brilliant that I thought it should hurt my eyes, but it didn't. There was a man waiting for us, and he showed us around. This was a great center for healing."

Helen Fredericks
Alhambra, California

"First of all, this was the clearest clairvoyant experience I have had since I first became interested in psychic abilities. It was the type of clear seeing that I had always dreamed of and programmed for. I saw a type of stone arched bridge with large columns on each side. I wondered what that was, and then the stone bridge turned into a modern bridge, like in San Francisco, and then back into the ancient bridge. On the bridge were several men in long white robes walking in line. I wondered who they were and a voice told me that they were high priests from Lemuria crossing over (to the area

now known as Sedona) to pray and raise their consciousness. And, in turn, Sedona's consciousness (energy)
would be raised by their presence. Next, I saw the priests
sitting in an area praying within a special design
imprinted in the red earth. In asking about the source of
the energy, I perceived large crystals beneath or inside
the rock formations."

J.S.
Chicago, IL

Not one to have my curiosity satisfied easily, I decided
to conduct the same experiment at each successive
Psychic Seminar to see whether the experiences
related by those in different groups would parallel those
of the initial experiment. The results were utterly
amazing! Not only did participants in each group
describe the same kinds of experiences, but the events
and images they perceived were nearly the same as the
groups who attended other seminars. Each seminar
group consisted of more than 150 people, so we now had
the results of several hundred participants, all describing
more or less the same types of images and situations.
What caused all these people to perceive the same
things?

As you read through the following reports, notice how
they compare to the reports from the first experiment.
Also notice how certain elements — crystals, unusual
energy sources, floods, healing — seem to come up again
and again. Not only are these themes repeated, but some
participants even describe similar details, such as
crystals aligned in certain patterns or underground
waterways and rivers:

"I was shown that the Sedona area was a 'staging
area' for the voluntary evacuation of the people of
Lemuria after the catastrophe that destroyed their

homeland on earth. I was shown a large round flat spaceship (some might say saucer) hovering over a flat-topped mesa, and being loaded with supplies for a long journey. I received the message, 'We came from space, and we are going home.'

"However, the Lemurians were given a choice whether to go or to stay here, and some chose to stay here. They eventually became the Hopi tribe. The crystals served as navigational aids as well as a power source for the airship. Many of them (crystals) were inside the mesa over which the airship hovered, and many others were scattered around in a planned pattern."

Patricia A. Sawyer
Derby, Kansas

"I saw two beams of light shooting out of the universe in a cross formation into the Sedona area. I felt entities of non-physical form arrive via these light beams. I identify myself and others in the seminar as reincarnations of these energies.

"The energies adopted a physical form on the earth plane. Their purpose: to teach a small group of humans living in the area. They failed in that they overstepped the boundaries of their mission and instead dominated the Sedona natives. The beings who came to Sedona had a certain aggressiveness to their personalities and yet I saw no overt acts of aggression. It was more that the natives, being a passive culture, more or less allowed the newly arrived entities to take command."

Melissa L. Applegate
Clearwater, Florida

"My first impressions were of drowning, of huge waves cascading over the marvelous red rocks with a thunderous noise. However, I quickly rose (floated) above this to a position of high overview whereby I immediately noticed a sky full of rainbows arching from one mesa to another all around me.

"'How beautiful,' I thought. And a voice answered, 'Yes, but ships do not fly on rainbows. Look, they have had to force land all over in valleys flooded with water. The energy flow has been disrupted.' And suddenly I could see the wreckage, the turmoil, the destruction.

"And the cave dwellers climbed out of the rock and called themselves 'blessed.' I do not see the cave dwellers as being of a high spiritual or mental nature. They were 'Keepers' only. I have been warned repeatedly not to search them out, that there was nothing in their contribution to this culture to emulate. They were simply 'what was left after the good souls departed.'"

Kathie Dame-Glerum
Sedona, Arizona

"I had been away from the Sedona area (perhaps off the earth, since the flooding surprised me). As I saw the canyon flooded about halfway to the top, I was convulsed with anguish for the lives that had been lost."

Adria Betty Elkins

"A Lemurian 'city' was here. It felt more like an information center. A large power pyramid made of energy was visible and rainbow-colored in the air over the Airport Vortex area. A wall, several hundred feet high and made of a smooth gray material, ran for miles on the east and north sides of the Sedona area. There were two runways that ran from a common point to the west. They seemed miles long. In the central part of the 'city' was a large wooded park with herds of animals.

"Under Bell Rock is a large crystal that sits upright. It is about or slightly below ground level, or where the base flares into the surrounding area. There is also a group of crystals buried under this whole area. They are in a distinct pattern but the crystals are pointing in random directions. This pattern covers hundreds of acres in each direction. Under the area—I've lost the location—is a metal container, like a time capsule, with information from then to now, from them to us. When I asked again about the connection, it still said a passing on or continuation of information."

Robert Spriggs

"The first image I got was of a lake with Indians in canoes; also a feeling of rather extensive submerged waterways used for communication/transportation of some kind. I also got an image/feeling of a huge time machine used for time travel or astronomical research. This was underground. In another underground area was one or more rooms used for magic."

R. H. W.
Woodland Hills, California

"This was not Lemuria. It is more ancient than Lemuria, which was situated nearer the Pacific Ocean. This is the most ancient place for entities from other planets to come to this earth. They are still coming. This energy is from time immemorial. You are here for you have all been a part of the growth of this planet, from this area as well as other places on the earth. Those who can stand in the light will remain, the others will become nothing. Acknowledge your inheritance and give thanks."

Diana Kruse
Aptos, California

"The Inner Temple was like a crystal cave. When the high priests were to enter a state of exteriorization, [*sic*] the higher realms they would visit would give them more insight and knowledge on how to handle the problems they encountered in the earth's dimension. The crystal cave seemed to impart a knowledge and healing effect. When the high priests would leave their earth bodies, they became as a light. The sounds inside the cave were like a finger stroking a thin crystal. The subdued sounds blended into the crystal vibration and created an atmosphere almost equal to the upper dimension."

Maxine Parker
Escondido, California

"I 'saw' the area's inhabitants actually enter into crystal spires to recharge themselves as one would recharge a battery. This was how they renewed energy, not by sleep."

Name Withheld
Burbank, California

"This crystal is somewhat like India's ruby, for it is located in a cave. Many know about the ruby, yet few venture to see it because, as the story goes, those with impure hearts who gaze upon the ruby lose their hearts. There are guardians at the entrance whose job it is to repel those of low (selfish) consciousness. The crystal illuminates so light isn't needed, though at this moment, the crystal is set on its right side instead of in its upright position. Water is provided on the third and lowest level. The small river flows from north to south. That which appears as a large stone is truly the door. Do not strike it, it will not open."

Rev. Dr. J. E. Arndt
Miami, Arizona

"The area is called Modalia. It is connected by a river to Chaco Canyon. It is a healing center."

Marion Durham
Flagstaff, Arizona

"In Boynton Canyon Vortex, I found a place where I could see no one, hear no one; it was as if I were totally alone in the world, yet I knew I was surrounded by an infinite number of souls. I meditated, as you taught us, for an hour. The sun moved warmly across my body. A sensuous breeze caressed my face. A bird talked to me. I was awash with peace. Not once did an insect bother me, though I had no netting nor had I used insect repellent. As I was coming out of meditation, viewing the mysterious and wonderful sight in front of me, everything seemed to shimmer and glow. I saw a brief but moving view: to the left, a brilliant, unearthly flash of light; to the right, I saw long, long boats filled with people. The boats were moving quickly. I felt a sense of urgency."

Name Withheld
Columbia, Missouri

"I went into trance at Bell Rock and saw many beautiful light beings 'popping' through an amazingly blue sky, each transporting a crystal. Each came to rest on a grassy meadow which was located in the Sedona area. I was one of the light beings and a crystal was in my keeping. I looked up and saw others 'popping' through and finally a **giant** crystal in the care of a great light being 'popped' through and I knew the task was at once finished and just begun. We were now waiting for the people to come in the boats from across the sea to begin our task.

"My vision changed to a scene of building. Dark-haired, dark-skinned people were working along with the light beings—a home, a place of safety, was being prepared for the crystals beneath the Earth—the surface of the Earth was not to be disturbed, or at least as little as possible. Great loving care was being exercised in this building. The dark-haired people had found homes in natural caves. Some of the light beings came to love the new land and the people so much they allowed themselves to be born into material existence, and so became caught in the cycle of karma—I was one of those."

Name Withheld
Topeka, Kansas

The following are excerpts of a three-page, single-spaced, typewritten letter I received from **Helen C. Fredericks** of **Alhambra, California**. She transcribed this extensively detailed message through automatic writing while in Boynton Canyon:

"Boynton Canyon is the center of the Inner City. Here is the purification center. Many Beings from other planets return to earth to merge with us to help, to center and to teach.

"When Lemuria sank into the Pacific, many had relocated. The Healing Center was transformed here. Caves were dug by use of crystals.

"This was a center for Healing and Rejuvenation. People of Lemuria traveled for years to attain the secrets of the crystals and the healers. Many beings, human and extraterrestrial who were once residents of Mu, are now being drawn back to the area for healing, rejuvenation and guidance.

"This will be the center of the coming age. Once again the people of Mu will switch frequency and lead the populace to peace, harmony and a high spirituality. The guidance is being received in many ways.

"What most beings, especially earth beings, do is

restrict the growth process. The people of Mu learned to expand those lessons with Freedom, the process of allowing each spirit to grow in any and all directions. Each must find his own center of his heart, of his spirit, and then follow it, while allowing everyone around him to follow his own heart.

"What happened since Mu was destroyed was the process of everyone having to conform, to believe the same, to follow someone else's spirit. How can someone believe or follow when they have no heart or spirit in the matter? There is a beauty in difference and this should be expanded, not controlled.

"Many do not know how to handle Freedom. This must be taught, for Freedom without responsibility is not Freedom, but a worse jail of the soul than restriction. The beauty of Freedom is the ability to Love unconditionally.

"Don't mourn the end of a civilization; celebrate the beginning of a new age, an age that not only allows change and difference, but encourages it.

"You ask of peace ... peace is everywhere, for it is contained in the soul of each of us. Most look for the physical peace of the outside world, like the peace and serenity of Boynton Canyon. But the same peace and serenity is within each being. One must start from the heart.

"The Inner City is now used as a monitoring center of earth. The large crystal controls all activity. The red earth carries the healing energies of the crystal to all who seek it. Each is drawn to the spot of frequency closest to their own.

"The maze of tunnels covers the whole area. The whole valley is a vortex, for the crystals are moved and worked in all areas. The workers of the Inner City use the crystals to heal the earth and those upon it. As the crystals are used, so they in turn are energized ... sort of a mutual exchange.

"Most rituals of healing are done in Boynton Canyon area. Communications are most successful at Bell Rock. Any of the vortexes may be used for assistance, but results are stronger in certain areas. One can ask for assistance from the Beings of the Inner City.

"Remember to always acknowledge the healing or communications came from God, or from the God-essence of oneself."

Chapter Five
"The Lost Continent of Mu"
By Gregory Frazier

"The Garden of Eden was not in Asia but on a now sunken continent in the Pacific Ocean. The Biblical story of creation—the epic of the seven days and the seven nights—came first not from the peoples of the Nile or of the Euphrates Valley but from this now submerged continent, Mu—the Motherland of Man."

Thus Colonel James Churchward (1852-1936) began the first in a series of five books about the ancient and mysterious sunken land of the Pacific, **The Lost Continent of Mu.**

In these books, Churchward claimed to have not only found the keys to unlock the mystery of the origin of man, but to have traced his ancient migrations to the four corners of the earth. Today there are those who believe that the Lemurian migrations eventually led to the American Southwest and the beautiful red-rock country surrounding present-day Sedona.

The name "Lemuria" was coined by scientists to describe the sunken mid-Pacific continent which was the original habitat of a far-ranging species of ape-like quadrupeds called lemurs. All ancient writings, however, refer to the lost continent as "Mu."

Churchward also pointed out some fascinating parallels connecting the inhabitants of Mu and certain Southwest Indian tribes. According to Churchward, these tribes are direct descendants of ancient Lemurians.

"I am not a professional archaeologist," Churchward wrote, "but I love the ancient and, for over fifty years, have been diligent in the study of it."

Born into an aristocratic Devonshire family, Church-ward was educated at Oxford and served in India as a colonel of a regiment of Bengal Lancers. At various times during his adventurous career, the tall, dashing Englishman was an explorer, big-game hunter, angler, inventor, tea planter, painter, civil engineer and racon-teur. He was also a Mason and reincarnationist who practiced telepathy and trance travel to former incarnations. Eventually, he settled in the United States, where he made—and later lost—a fortune in the steel business.

As a young man serving in India as a double agent for British Intelligence, he had occasion to visit a monas-tery. There he met an old rishi whom he described as a "great master, the last surviving member of the ancient Naacal priesthood."

The rishi eventually led Churchward to a hidden cave and a cache of ages-old clay tablets. The tablets were written in Naacal, the rishi explained, the oldest language of man. They told of the geology, history and religion of Mu the Motherland, and its cataclysmic destruction over 12,000 years earlier.

"He taught me how to **learn** to read ancient writings and inscriptions," Churchward wrote in **The Children of Mu.** "It was a hobby of his and mine also."

Churchward wrote the first edition of **The Lost Con-tinent of Mu** based on his interpretation of the Naacal tablets. He later revised the book after interpreting another series of 12,000-year-old tablets discovered beginning in 1921 by mineralogist William Niven in the Valley of Mexico. Together, the Naacal and Niven tablets provided the foundation of Churchward's hypothesis.

According to Churchward and other Mu historians, Mu comprised an area of some 180,000 square miles. The Pacific islands are believed to be Lemurian mountain tops. When devastating earthquakes sunk Lemuria on

Friday the 13th Day of Zac, 64 million souls were drowned, an end to 200 millennia of development.

Wishar S. Cervé, in his book, **Lemuria—The Lost Continent of the Pacific**, described the typical Lemurian as a tall, well-muscled vegetarian who was far advanced mentally and spiritually. In the center of his high forehead was a growth about the size of a walnut. This "third eye" was actually the Lemurian's sixth sense organ. Through it, he could see, hear, feel and communicate over long distances. He was also capable of communicating with animals, and could "see" into the fourth dimension.

The Lemurians possessed powerful magnetic stones or crystals, found in volcanic areas, which radiated energy and light. These crystals had the strange ability to repel water and were used to power the boats which ultimately brought the Lemurians to North America.

Lemurian religion was based on fact, as opposed to faith, containing no sects, theologies or dogma. All Lemurians were attuned to the Cosmic Mind or Consciousness, which permeates the universe.

Reincarnation, an established fact to the Lemurians, was the crux of their religion. "In the Sacred Writings of Mu," Churchward wrote, "we are told man's soul lives on until finally it reaches the source of its origin."

About 70,000 years before the destruction of Mu, a colonial movement began sending groups of migrations westward to Asia and eastward to South, Central and North America. The first of these eastern migrations led to approximately the present state of Nevada at a time preceding the rising of our western mountain ranges.

As evidence of the Lemurian presence in the Southwest, Churchward offers geographic, linguistic, symbolic and religious data gathered from various Indian tribes: the Nootka of British Columbia, the Mound Builders of the Southeast, the Pueblo Indians (Hopi and Zuni), and the Cliff Dwellers of the Southwest. The Cliff Dwellers were the last to arrive.

"Working inland from the Colorado River's mouth, they would first pass through Arizona, which state is full of their remains," Churchward explained. "Their old homes and remains show that they worked out on the Gila, Little Colorado and Grand Rivers."

Montezuma Castle National Monument, an Arizona cliff dwelling, is located just a few miles from Sedona. Also nearby is the Tuzigoot National Monument, a stone pueblo where hundreds of Indians lived between 1100-1400 A.D. Were the inhabitants of these dwellings Lemurians or descendants of the Lemurians?

According to Churchward, there were at least four civilizations occupying Arizona and the Southwest **before** the cliff dwellers and the present-day Indians. "It is quite possible that the actual Cliff Dwellers and the red Indians may be races that have descended from remnants that were saved during the raising of the mountains," he theorized. He points to their writings on boulders and cliffs which contain symbols similar to those found on the Naacal and Niven tablets.

"That the Cliff Dwellers came from Mu is certain," Churchward wrote, "for every one of their pictures that are used for guideposts contains a reference to Mu. In fact, the rock writings and pictures of the Cliff Dwellers, except those drawn for artistic effects, are permeated with references to Mu, both before and after her submersion. In addition to this, they invariably used the symbols that were in vogue in the Motherland."

Churchward investigated several interesting parallels between the Hopi and Zuni cultures and that of Lemuria. He believed that these Indian tribes were highly developed and enlightened people at the time of their arrival in the Southwest.

"Various Pueblo traditions, their language, their sacred symbols and other evidences *prove that the Pueblo Indians originally came to America from Mu.*" [*Editor's Note: The italics are Churchward's.*]

Particularly fascinating is Quetzalcoatl, the bearded serpent, symbol of Creation, which is common to the Pueblos, Mayas, Aztecs—and Lemurians. One of the Niven tablets, discovered at a grave site in Guerrero, Mexico, was interpreted by Churchward as follows: "Quetzalcoatl ... called him, and his soul passed on to the region of darkness (submerged Mu) there to await the call from the great serpent for reincarnation." And this: "When Quetzalcoatl ... calls—the eyes of those closed in sleep are opened, the time of their reincarnation has arrived. They answer the call of the Great Serpent and come forth into a new day."

Could Mu be the limbo of dead souls, waiting for their moment of reincarnation?

Hopi Indian legend would seem to support Churchward's hypothesis. The Hopis believe they originally came out of the west on bamboo rafts. Arriving at a wall of steep mountains, they climbed to the top and looked back; in the distance, they could see islands sinking. The continent of Mu consisted of one large and two smaller islands.

The Hopis are a deeply religious culture with many magic-oriented beliefs—as were the Lemurians. Beneath their dwellings, the Hopis dig kivas, underground rooms used for religious ceremonies. The Lemurians also used underground rooms for religious rites.

The Indians consider the Sedona red-rock country to be sacred ground; the home of the Great Spirit. Perhaps this is why so many people in search of enlightenment and

65

inner peace come to this area, attracted, as it were, by some invisible force. Visitors from the ethereal plane are also said to linger here.

Amazing psychic occurrences have been reported as well: visions, telepathy, past-life regressions, precognitions, UFO sightings, poltergeist activity, enhanced automatic writing, spiritual healings, and other psychic phenomena.

An ancient Lemurian city is said to be buried beneath the Cococino sandstone. Powerful talisman-like crystals are thought to be hidden underground. (Coincidentally, the Navajo Indians believe that they emerged from underground.)

This testimony isn't surprising, considering that Sedona is one of the world's three most powerful energy centers. Surrounding Sedona are four energy vortexes— two electric, one magnetic, and one electromagnetic— more than any other single spot on earth!

Unseen forces are constantly at work all around us. Every physical object on earth—organic and inorganic— gives off electromagnetic radiation. The effects of these unseen forces are little understood. What is understood, however, is that electromagnetic fields **do affect** living organisms. Metabolism, heart rate, body temperature, blood pressure, as well as the visual, aural and tactile senses are affected by electromagnetism. Experiments with monkeys have shown, for example, that when the monkey's head is placed in an electromagnetic field tuned to alpha, its brain waves will begin to pulse in synchronization with the alpha rate.

In other words, truth and reality exist on many different levels. The parallels between ancient Lemuria and modern Sedona certainly deserve further investigation—on all levels. Given the awesome natural beauty of the Sedona red-rock country, perhaps we should heed the rishi's parting words to the young Churchward:

"Go forth into the world, my son, and learn that which is written by nature. Nature is the great schoolhouse provided for man in which to learn. Nature does not theorize. Nature does not lie. Nature is truth personified. ... Every rock has a tale written on its wrinkled and weathered face, and the tales are true. Every blade of grass, every leaf on tree and shrub has a whisper for listening ears...."

Chapter Six
"Ley Lines Link Sedona To All Earth's Power Spots"
By Kathie Dame-Glerum

I n China, they are known as Dragon Currents, in Ireland as Fairy Paths, in the Americas as Serpent Power. The Aborigines in Australia refer to a "line of songs." And in England, the ley line systems are referred to simply as the Old Straight Track.

Ley lines are lines of natural magnetic currents—alignments of prehistoric sites and natural landmarks. A number of ley lines mark some extreme position of the sun or moon. Frequently, they are ancient roads or pathways, clearly visible from the air; sometimes they are only briefly visible as shadows or light paths.

Locating ley line energy was an ancient art not unlike that of dowsing with divining rods; a carefully taught science handed down through magicians, Druidic priests in the early mystery schools, and Chinese geomancers. The job of the geomancer was to interpret the earth in terms of the heavens, to detect currents and assess their influence on the land. Migrating birds, following lines of magnetic current, were often studied.

Ley lines are marked by giant earthworks and mounds in the American Midwest; by dirt roadways leading from Chaco Canyon, New Mexico, to Teotihuacan, Mexico; by a series of long, straight tracks emanating from Cuzco, the old Inca capital high in the Peruvian Andes which is associated in local tradition with a primeval, god-like race; by lines criss-crossing the Nazca plains of Peru—lines with great astrological significance, oriented in such a way as to predict equinoxes and solstices. And they are marked by visible lines tying together every

69

major religious site in Britain, from Stonehenge to the legendary Glastonbury Tor, home of King Arthur, Merlin and the Holy Grail.

Every early Christian church was sited along the flow of ley line current, the greatest energy located directly beneath the tower to produce the strongest fusion of heaven and earth.

The Dragon Currents of China mark all sacred paths and centers throughout that country. These currents are divided into those of yin and yang, positive and negative, the currents of the White Tiger and the Blue Dragon. The Chinese believe that the dragon pulse—the energy vortex—is at its peak where the yin of gently undulating country meets the yang of sharp rocks and peaks, particularly if this site is quiet and sheltered and secluded, as is much of Sedona.

Sedona is noted world-wide for its high concentration of active energy and power. The residents will often speak of a "genii loci." Sedona spelled backwards is "anodes": in an electrolytic cell, the positively charged electrode towards which current flows; in an electron tube, the principal electrode for collecting electrons. Also, according to Webster's, "a way up." Perhaps this is indeed what Sedona provides. It is the only spot on earth to contain four major vortexes within a few square miles.

A vortex is a high concentration of energy, a receiving station for direct influences; by definition, a state resembling a whirlpool. It is surrounded by grids—a similar energy field that is not yet centered—where ley lines share a common point of intersection.

The vortex areas have been likened to acupressure points on the body. In a similar manner, grids can be compared to the nervous system. At the point where these are concentrated, as in Sedona, emotions run high.

Things happen at these points first—on the earth's body as well as on our own. Together, they form a sacred geometric pattern across the earth with universal repercussions.

Like attracts like; therefore, electrical vortexes will be connected via ley lines or electrical currents—to other electrical vortexes. In Sedona, the Bell Rock and Airport Road vortexes are connected to other major electrical vortexes on Mt. Everest, Mt. Ararat in Eastern Turkey and Mt. McKinley (Denali) in Alaska. The magnetic vortex at Cathedral Rock is connected to the major magnetic vortex of Glastonbury Tor in Britain, another recognized site of great regeneration.

As you meditate in any of the vortexes in the Sedona area, you are tying into a universal energy pattern of astounding magnitude and not just one particular energy facet. And the key seems to lie in certain sound combinations reverberating throughout the universal ley line system: in humming, as reported by guides in certain chambers of the Great Pyramids; in the legendary song of the Sirens; in chanting heard by those who have remained quiet long enough while deep into Boynton Canyon. The Healing Circles of Dick Sutphen, held in Sedona, are extremely powerful; the vibrations of the "OM" chant combining with the human magnetism of the group and resounding in a universal spirit of love and healing physically felt.

The ley line system has always meant healing, the renewal of the life force. The lines themselves become animated at certain seasons of the year by a vital force, a rejuvenating influence that can be drawn through the earth. And the direction of its flow varies with the phases of the moon.

From time immemorial, ancient rites have been performed on the ley lines throughout the earth within arrangements of carved dots and stone circles to ensure

71

the return of this force—from the Druids of Britain and the Aborigines of Australia to the Quiche Maya of South America. The Hopi Indians use the lines as cables of mental communication. It is said that stone can be levitated by sound along the ley lines of magnetic intensity, the level of intensity altered by tone and pitch.

The late Dr. Wilhelm Reich in **The Discovery of the Orgone** proved the existence of this pure life force, which he called orgone energy, by storing and channeling it to produce dramatic changes in the weather with the use of a simple apparatus. He felt, by using the ley line system, even space travel was possible with the flow of inter-galactic currents of energy.

It seems only logical to believe that there was, long ago, a universal civilization with an advanced knowledge of science and magic. A magic based on numbers, which unified all the individual arts and sciences, customs, folklore, mythology, monuments and cultures universally. It is a physical fact that the prehistoric sites fall into perfectly straight alignments when shown on a map. And all these sites were mathematically equated and built with extraordinary precision. The actual key to all these ancient and natural sites seems to lie in numbers.

The vibrational force of the ley line/vortex/grid system in Sedona is the number seven. As Sedona is said to be built over an ancient Lemurian city, it is interesting to note that seven is also the number of Lemuria.

From the beginning of time, the mystical code of numbers and vibrations, translated into sound and light patterns, has been at the root of all ancient knowledge and belief. And the ley line/vortex/grid system has been the power by which it is transferred. There is a oneness to be felt with the universe which seems to come more easily in a vortex or healing circle in Sedona. And a responsibili-ty to return that which is given—knowledge and spirit...and peace

*　　*　　*

Another explanation for these power spots was put forth by C. W. Leadbeater, one of the early leaders of the Theosophical Society. In 1910, he authored a two-volume set of books titled **The Inner Life**. The books present a general overview of the entire metaphysical belief structure. In a chapter about the work of the Masters, he explains that nineteen-hundred years ago, the White Brotherhood sent a man upon a mission to establish magnetic centers in various countries:

> Objects of the nature of talismans were given to him, which he was to bury at these chosen spots, in order that the force which they radiated might prepare these places to be the centers of great events in the future.

Another interesting quote from the same book:

> Masters frequently take advantage of special occasions and of places where there is some strong magnetic center. They cause Their own force to radiate along the channels which are already prepared. When some vast assemblage of pilgrims comes together in a receptive attitude, again They take advantage of the occasion by pouring Their forces out upon the people through the channels by means of which they have been taught to expect help and blessing.

Perhaps this explains the enormous psychic impact Sedona has on both the aware and the unaware and those who have attended **Psychic Seminars** here.

Chapter Seven
Vortex Locations and Warnings

In this chapter, I will give you the exact locations of the four primary vortexes with detailed explanations of how to reach them. In addition, I will share with you some very important information you need to know before experiencing these very intense vibrational fields.

First, I want to make a very strong point about the spirituality of the vortex areas, especially the Boynton Canyon area. As you read in previous chapters, the area is considered sacred by the Yavapai. When you enter here, have the same respect you would as if you were entering a place of worship, for that's what it is. Even now, you may encounter Indians here; they still travel from the cities and reservations to regularly observe their religious practices in the canyon. If you should come upon Indians worshipping in the area, please move quietly away so as not to disturb them. Don't stand around and gawk.

Because of all the recent development, especially at the mouth of Boynton Canyon, it has been increasingly difficult for the Indians, especially the elders who are not as agile, to gain access to these sacred areas. Attempts are being made to improve access to the canyon. Supposedly, a new trail is now being constructed. We should support every effort to make access to the sacred areas easier for the Indian people and to avoid disturbing them while we pursue our own worship and meditations.

Please be extremely respectful in every way while experiencing the vortex area; this includes taking out everything that you carry in, from cigarette butts to any drink containers. I'm especially concerned about the ecology, but beyond that, you don't want to upset the spirits that reside here.

Also, remember that Arizona is rattlesnake country. Wear hiking boots, or even better, high-topped boots such as cowboy boots. The only problem with cowboy boots is that they are terrible for climbing if you plan to scale any of the higher areas. Extensive climbing is really unnecessary to experience any of the vortex areas, but you may want to climb just for the experience or for another view of the beautiful surrounding country. There is little concern about rattlesnakes in the winter months, for they are hibernating, but as the weather becomes warmer, the risk of running into rattlesnakes becomes greater. In the spring, the snakes will often come out to warm themselves on the rocks; in the summer months, they can be a real problem. Never, never, never walk through grass where you don't have a full view of the surrounding ground—snakes will often be under rocks or brush. Make plenty of noise as you walk; this will give the snakes a chance to get out of your way. They don't want to confront you any more than you want to confront them.

In my years of exploring the Arizona desert areas, I've had at least 25 encounters with snakes, and I must stress the importance of being aware. Never, under any circumstances while climbing or moving through the rocks, place your hand in a position that you can't see. Climbers pulling themselves up the rocks have reached up to grab hold and have been struck in the hand, or worse yet, pulled themselves up to a ledge or shelf only to come face to face with a coiled snake.

It is best to work with someone else in the vortex areas in the warmer months because of the snakes. Take along a blanket or pad to sit or lie on if you plan to explore in an altered state of consciousness. Place it in an open area away from piles of rocks and underbrush. While one person is in trance, the other can watch over them. They can also be of assistance, as I'll describe later.

Also, never sleep in a sleeping bag on the open ground anywhere in Arizona. If you plan to camp, bring along a closed tent or a cot that will keep you off the ground. Rattlesnakes are known to slither down into a sleeping bag to share the warmth generated by the inhabitant's body heat. All will be fine until you desire to crawl out of the bag, which might upset the snake.

Please don't allow the discussion of rattlesnakes to keep you from experiencing the vortex areas or to do so in a paranoid state. If you keep in mind what I've told you, your chances of encountering a snake are extremely rare. I just don't want you blundering across the Arizona landscape as if you were in a park in the city. Be aware that the desert is the snakes' home, not yours.

If you should encounter a coiled snake, rattling its tail, freeze immediately; judge the situation and, if appropriate, back slowly away. The snake is capable of striking only its own length, but five-foot rattlers aren't rare in this area. If you are struck, get away instantly, for a rattler will strike again and again as long as its prey is within reach, and the first strike carries only a small amount of venom in comparison to the second, when the snake's system is fully pumping the poison. Most Arizonans carry a snake-bite kit when in the back country. They are readily available in local stores.

The very latest information on snake bites indicates that if you are bitten and immediately take large doses of Vitamin C, in either the form of crystals or a fast-acting formula, it seems to negate the effects of the venom. However, if bitten, you should always go **immediately** to a hospital.

It is also wise to be aware that scorpions inhabit the area. Their bite is not deadly for most people, but it is painful and can make you sick. Scorpions usually hide under rocks and deadwood, or between the cracks in rocks. Be careful that you do not sit down on rocks containing open cracks. Scorpions, unlike snakes, are not a bit wary of people, and have been known to walk right up to a person and bite him.

Another warning I feel is important is in regard to the inner voices that empathic people are known to have experienced in the vortex areas. A good friend, who knows the Boynton Canyon area like the back of his hand, found himself following the voices. He climbed high up into the rocks and crevices, only to get himself into a position that required every bit of climbing skill he possessed to get himself safely down. The slightest slip, and he could have fallen to his death.

Seminar participant **John C. Harriman** of **Lynn, Massachusetts,** had a similar experience when he went to the Airport Mesa Vortex late one night:

"When I was first told about Sedona, it came to mind that a certain gift should be brought ... a piece of jade. I went to the Airport Mesa; it was around ten o'clock at night and pitch black. Parking my car and grabbing my flashlight, I started the climb up.

"After walking for a few minutes, a voice said to me, 'Turn off the light, you will not need it.' So I did as I was instructed. It was dark, but I could see with no problem at all and continued to climb.

"Several times I heard rocks clattering, as if a person had stepped and moved a rock in doing so. Being an avid outdoorsman, I knew it was not an animal—it was a two-legged creature, not a four-legged one. And, as I stated earlier, I could see in the dark.

"Eventually, I reached the top and walked to the edge, which I could see with no problem. It was at the very top of the Mesa where I knew I was supposed to leave the jade. But I wanted to be absolutely sure. So I said, 'I will leave it tomorrow after going to Courthouse and Boynton Canyon Vortices.' (*Editor's Note: He had already been to the Bell Rock Vortex earlier.*]

"It was like a voice saying, 'No, leave it here.' I said, 'No, tomorrow,' and continued down the Mesa.

"I stepped on a rock, and it was as though it just jumped out from under my right foot. Well, needless to say, I fell and banged my left knee. And a voice said, 'Leave the jade.' I said, 'No, I'll leave it tomorrow.'

"The reason I wanted to hold onto the jade is that I wanted to go to the other Vortices and see if I got a stronger inclination to leave the jade someplace else.

"After a few minutes of pain—I didn't swear or cuss—I got up and continued. I brushed a cactus and got quite a few thorns in my left leg. And again a voice said, 'Leave the jade.' Again, I said, 'No, I'll leave it tomorrow.'

"A few minutes later, something stopped me. Something just wasn't right. I looked again and it looked as though I were at the edge of a rim. I turned on my flashlight and, sure enough, I was on the edge of a rim with a parking lot in front of me. If I had continued without stopping, I would have fallen about eight feet."

Remember, spirits can be of lower as well as higher vibrations. Whenever you contact spirit voices in meditation, automatic writing, self-hypnosis or any other altered state, use your own intuition in evaluating what they have to say. In general, your guides or good spirits do just that—they "guide" you. If you ever encounter voices or written suggestions "demanding" that you do something, beware! Not all entities are working in your best interests. Trust your own feelings and good sense as to whether you should do as they suggest.

As in these two cases, voices telling you to climb to a dangerous or inaccessible location, (even with the "promise" of some kind of reward or discovery), or to climb a mountain in the dark, or do anything that you would ordinarily consider unsafe to do, or that could be physically, mentally or emotionally destructive, are probably of a malevolent nature. Ignore them. And, as an added protection, imagine yourself surrounded with the white God light. Don't let the experiences override common sense. Even if you know the back country, Arizona is unique and you need considerable survival skills and adequate water and supplies to explore safely.

There are many ancient Indian caves in the area, and if you dig in any of these, you are subject to a fine of several thousand dollars and a term in prison. There are also very stringent laws about digging up any of the cactuses or plants on park land and public property. I also feel it is very bad luck to remove any rocks from the vortex areas without permission of the spirits, attained while in meditation.

And remember that some of the vortex areas are on private property and the owners may take a dim view of your explorations.

THE VORTEX LOCATIONS

After describing the exact locations of the vortexes, I'll tell you my own ways of testing the energy and activating and expanding upon it for your own subjective explorations. I'll begin all my directions from the center of Sedona at the junction of Highways 89A and 179. Directions are well-marked at the intersection. If you follow 89A toward Flagstaff, you'll drive up the switchbacks through Oak Creek Canyon. This is one of the most beautiful drives on earth, although no major vortex areas are located in this direction. If you follow 89A west toward Cottonwood and Jerome, you are moving in the proper direction for the Airport Mesa Vortex and the

Boynton Canyon Area Vortex. All visitors will want to make the trip to Jerome, which takes about 40 minutes. This is the largest ghost town in the country and once was a thriving mining area. Today, many craftsmen have moved back here, repairing some of the deteriorating homes and have opened shops and restaurants.

If you take Highway 179 out of town, it will lead you past Tlaquepaque, the beautiful Spanish Colonial shopping and craft center. Past Tlaquepaque and on out 179 toward Black Canyon Freeway, which is Interstate 17, you'll come to the Bell Rock Vortex and the turn-off to the Courthouse Rock Vortex.

I will give you the mileage points as they register on your car's odometer, but remember that some odometers may register a little differently, depending upon the size of your tires, so keep this variant in mind when following these instructions.

I've included a little map of the area to make finding the vortexes much easier, but a map is not necessary if you follow these instructions exactly. Everything I'll relate is accurate at the time of this printing, and although the vortexes and the main roads won't change, some road signs, change in property ownership and new constructions can alter circumstances.

For instance, you used to be able to drive in quite close to most of the vortexes, but recently the National Park Service has put up fences blocking the roads into these areas and is constructing parking lots, probably because of the increasing amounts of visitors to these spiritual locations. So, although you'll have to walk farther to get to the vortexes, parking should be less of a problem than it has been in the past.

Where you used to be able to drive up to the base of Bell Rock, now you have to stop about one-eighth of a mile away. At Red Rock Crossing, near Courthouse Rock, you'll have to hike about half a mile. There are now two new parking lots there.

Before I describe the exact locations of the four primary vortexes, let me just reiterate the types of positive vortexes found in Sedona and the kind of energy they radiate. Positive vortexes are charged in one of three ways:

Electric: These are "yang," charged with the male force. When you enter the vibrational field or frequency, you will become charged emotionally and physically. The energy will stimulate and elevate consciousness. It is also ideal to eliminate depression. Some people consider an electrical vortex to be a strain on someone with high blood pressure or heart problems.

Magnetic: These are "yin," charged with the female force. When you enter the vibrational field or frequency, you can expect to open psychically, becoming much more perceptive, for the effects are primarily on the subconscious mind.

Electromagnetic: These vortexes are a combination of electrical and magnetic—or a combination of the yin-yang forces, resulting in a perfect state of balance. When you enter the vibrational field or frequency, you can expect an expansion and elevation of consciousness. This energy is ideal to stimulate past-life memories and psychic activities.

Bell Rock (An Electric Vortex). Location: From the intersection of Highways 89A and 179, drive out of Sedona on 179 toward Black Canyon Freeway, which is Interstate 17. Drive 5.1 miles on 179; on the left-hand side of the road is Bell Rock. It is impossible to miss; it is a huge, bell-shaped red rock that sits just off the highway on your left.

This is purported to be a "beacon vortex"; it is said that the energy emits from the base and out the top, extending

82

miles into the air. This may explain why there have been so many UFO sightings above Bell Rock over the years. Those desiring to experience the energy of Bell Rock Vortex would have to be right at, or up on, the base. Because it is electric, being within the frequency should stimulate consiousness. Due to the beacon-like quality, psychics report that the location is excellent for communication with higher forms of life.

Airport Mesa (An Electric Vortex). Location: From the intersection of Highways 89A and 179, drive 1.1 miles toward Cottonwood and turn left at Airport Road. Go up Airport Road four-tenths of a mile. The "Cattle Guard" sign that used to be here is gone, but on the right side of the road is a sign saying "Rainbow Ray Focus." Not far away is a pull-off area on the right. The trail to the vortex is on your left, about halfway between the sign and the pull-off area. There are a couple of rough trails that lead up the hill.

Please be aware that unless your car is completely off the road, they will tow it away, and there is only enough room for a few cars to pull off. So, if other people are in the area, park your car and walk up to the area.

Once you've come to the top of the hill, you'll walk down into the vortex area. It is approximately half a block long and stops at a cliff that looks down on the valley below. This is the vortex I wrote about in one of my books. Because it is electric in nature, it can be expected to charge you emotionally and physically while also elevating consciousness.

Courthouse Rock (A Magnetic Vortex). Location: From the intersection of Highways 89A and 179, drive out of Sedona on 179 toward Black Canyon Freeway, which is Interstate 17. You'll come to The Village of Oak Creek, and when your odometer reads 7.2 miles, turn right on Verde Valley School Road. Continue for another 3.2 miles

and you'll see Courthouse Rock as the huge rock formation on your right, several blocks from the road. This is
the closest you can get to the rock without a four-wheel-
drive vehicle. And, although Courthouse Rock is the
most photographed rock formation in the area, this view
is the least desirable. If you want to view it at its best,
continue on down Verde Valley School Road for another
2.1 miles until the road dead-ends into Oak Creek. You
can also walk in from this point, which is more scenic but
is a greater distance.

The vortex energy emanations are said to extend from
Courthouse Rock to about 500 yards around the base.
Because it is magnetic in nature, you can expect the
activation of your subconscious mind, becoming more
psychic, and stimulating forgotten memories, past lives,
and so on.

Because the Courthouse is "yin" charged, some people
are concerned that it emits negative energy. On one level,
yin denotes negative, but this certainly is not the kind of
negativity you would experience in a negative vortex
area such as the Bermuda Triangle. The yin energy of
Courthouse Rock could be likened to the positive and
negative energy in an automobile battery. A battery
consists of alternating positive- and negative-charged
plates. It is the alternating interaction of the two that
generates the energy that you use to start your car and
power the electrical components. The negative plate isn't
"bad," any more than the positive plate is "good." All
structures require the yin/yang interaction to exist.
Human beings are also structures.

**Boynton Canyon Area (An Electromagnetic Vor-
tex).** Location: From the intersection of Highways 89A
and 179, drive toward Cottonwood, Arizona, 3.2 miles,
until you come to Dry Creek Road on the right. Also at
the intersection, on the right, is a metaphysical

bookstore called "The Golden Word," for those who are interested. Turn right and proceed down Dry Creek Road another 2.9 miles until the road forks. At this point, turn left following the signs directing you toward Boynton Pass; go another 1.6 miles until the road forks again. Turn right following the Boynton Canyon sign. If you go down this road four-tenths of a mile, you will see a very small **firebreak** road off to the right. Stop here. If you look down the main road another one-tenth of a mile, you'll see a gate which is the entrance to a new private resort home area that is under development. This development covers 70 acres and blocks the direct entrance to Boynton Canyon. This private land covers an area between the canyon walls approximately half a mile from the gate back into the canyon. If you are individuals, and obviously not camping, the resort may allow you to pass through the area, but you'll have to check with the office and the gate is usually locked on the weekends as of the time of this printing. There is a watchman who patrols the area with a shotgun, so please don't violate private property without permission. Besides, it is unnecessary, for the road through this property only extends half a mile.

Boynton Canyon is a box canyon, but the energy appears to be centered from the back of the canyon. Only a large vertical rock formation separates the energy center from an extension of the canyon and you can easily get behind it by using the firebreak road.

So, let's go back to the point where you stopped at the firebreak road. To the best of my knowledge, this is park land, as is most of the land in this area. The firebreak road is now closed to all vehicles. Park off the main road and begin to walk, following the firebreak road for three-fourths of a mile. This will take you right into the most beautiful, awesome canyon area you probably have ever seen. As you walk down the firebreak road, at about the half-mile point, off to your left, you will begin to see smooth, sheer red-rock walls ascending over a thousand feet into the air. You can go back as far into the canyon as you want, but you'll have to make your way through the scrub, high-desert growth, which is very easy to do.

The Boynton Canyon Area Vortex is my favorite of the Sedona area vortexes. You don't even have to be psychically sensitive to experience the tremendous power here. This is also the largest vortex in the area, with energy emitting from the ground for several miles in every direction. Some people feel even more strongly about the canyon that lies next to the Boynton on your left as you are walking in. If you want to experience that area, you can go back four-tenths of a mile to the point where you turned right and continue down the road approximately one mile until you have another chance to turn right.

The Boynton Canyon Area is called "sacred ground" by many locals. It is a sacred area to the Yavapai Indians, who say it is the home of the "Great Mother," which they perceive as the creative force. Because the area is electromagnetic, it is perfectly balanced and will expand and elevate consciousness. It should stimulate all subconscious memories (past lives) and your psychic abilities should be greatly enhanced here.

Chapter Eight
Vortex Experiments

Y ou now have the four locations. And before I go into testing the energy and working in an altered state of consciousness, let me give you another tip that may very well make your vortex journey much more enjoyable. As with any outside location, especially in warm months, the vortexes will have some bugs and flies. Since you will be attempting to meditate or induce self-hypnosis, you'll need to be able to totally focus your attention upon subjective input without distractions, so bring a good insect repellent or some cheesecloth or fine netting to place over your body while in trance.

Now, let's discuss how to test, activate and expand the vortex energy to maximize the psychic potential of your vortex experience. First, if you conduct your subjective explorations in an altered state of consciousness, even if it is only a very light altered state, you are sure to be more successful, for you have easier access to subconscious awareness and memories when you are in alpha or theta brain levels. A deeper trance will assist you in accessing the higher self or superconscious mind. This is certainly most desirable for contacting the other side or higher forms of life.

I'm sure most people interested in this book have already developed their own altered-state techniques, and if so, use what you are familiar with. If you are new to using an altered state of consciousness, which means meditation or self-hypnosis, simply follow these easy instructions: To begin, make yourself comfortable in a sitting or prone position, then take at least 10 very deep breaths. The yoga breathing technique has you take a very deep breath in and hold it as long as possible. Then let the breath out slowly through slightly parted teeth. This allows you to retain moisture in your mouth and thus be more comfortable. When you think the breath is all the way out, contract your stomach muscles and force the breath farther and farther out. Then breathe in and repeat the process. When you inhale using this technique, your diaphragm cuts in even before your lungs and it is very relaxing. So take at least 10 of these deep breaths—even more if you need them to calm down. While doing your deep breathing, begin to quiet your mind and focus your attention strictly upon the breathing process. You want to allow the quietness of spirit to begin to come in.

Next, mentally begin to relax your body one part at a time, beginning with your feet and moving up your legs into your hands, forearms and upper arms. Then relax the base of your spine, and move the relaxing power up your spine and into the back of your neck and shoulder muscles. The relaxing power is then to move up your neck into your scalp and drain down into your facial muscles. As you think about each part of your body relaxing, play the role, play the part, and really feel the relaxing sensations coming into your body.

The next step is to imagine a beam of bright, white light coming down from above and beginning to flow through your body and mind. This is the white God light of protection. Make this image real and create the light with the unlimited power of your mind. Next, imagine the light concentrating around your heart area and then emerging from your heart area to surround your body with a protective, magnetic aura of bright, white God light. Personally, I also like to recite the following invocation of protection while I'm surrounding myself in this spiritual aura:

To Thee, God, be the kingdom and the power
and the glory unto the ages of ages ... Amen. I

seek thy protection from all things seen and unseen, all forces and all elements. In Thy divine name, I open to the light. I offer my body, my mind and my spirit to the light. Let Thy divine will and mine be as one. I seek to expand the light within and I seek a tranquil mind and harmony with the divine law. I thank Thee in advance for the unfolding visions, spiritual awareness and healing that await me. As it is above, so it is below. I ask these things in Thy name. I beseech it and I mark it ... and so it is.

Once the protection is complete, imagine yourself going down into a peaceful meditative state while you slowly count backward from 50 to one. While you are counting, vividly fantasize yourself climbing from the top of one of the beautiful red rocks slowly and safely down to the bottom. When you reach the number one, you will be in an altered state of consciousness.

Of course, the more you use an altered state, the more conditioned you become ... and the better you are conditioned, the more likely you will be to have vivid experiences in the vortex area.

Once you are ready to awaken, all you have to do is count yourself up from one to five and say the words, "wide awake, wide awake."

Now, let's talk about how to experience the vortex energy while in an altered state. Once you've completed the countdown, slowly raise your hands, palms down, a few inches above the earth, and attempt to feel the energy. Your mind must be relaxed and focused only upon the feelings in your hands. Many people report great tingling in their hands, or that they begin to feel lighter and lighter, which is the energy pushing up out of the ground.

If you're on the edge of the vortex, hold your hands palms out toward the vortex area, and again, feel the energy. Then reverse the direction, palms away from the vortex area, and you'll feel much less energy. This experiment will work best if you're sitting at the top of the Airport Mesa Vortex before entering the actual vortex area. It will also work if you remain a distance from Bell Rock or Courthouse Rock. There is simply too much energy coming up out of the ground for miles around Boynton Canyon for this experiment to work well. You'll feel the energy no matter what direction you face.

Now, here are some additional experiments that, for many, greatly increase and expand the energy. The first is with a crystal, or crystal pendulum, which is readily available from most metaphysical bookstores. Go into an altered state with the crystal on your third-eye area, in the center of your forehead. Conduct the experiments I've already described, or use it to open for psychic impressions or ask to receive past-life information. I'll explain more about how to do this shortly. Another variation of this technique is to place the crystal upon your psychic-center acupressure point. This point can be easily found by running your finger down the center of your chest until you come to the bottom of your rib cage. The point where the bone ends is the psychic center. Again, conduct the experiments or seek subjective input.

Crystals amplify body energy and thoughts. Many people use them to focus their energy. Crystals create power and clarity in thinking, and since the vortex opens you psychically and stimulates the subconscious, you can expect some vivid experiences. The crystal will also amplify the energy of the vortex.

Two variations of these experiments are to use a small pyramid or a small vortex rock in exactly the same manner as I've described with the crystals. Because we all differ vibrationally, not everyone will experience the same things—each person will have unique results with different techniques in the vortexes.

I've had people tell me they have had their most vivid experiences when in the vortex area during a full moon or at the time of the new moon. Recent medical studies have shown that both these phases of the moon have a profound and measurable effect upon a great many people. Again, though, the effect can be negative as well as positive, so the energy of the vortex could exaggerate the negativity.

As is often the case when exploring astral projection, some people exploring vortex energy prefer to remove their clothes and all jewelry, then lie down with their heads facing north. You'll have to judge the appropriateness of this technique for yourself. If you do desire to explore it, I'd suggest you find a secluded place in the Boynton Canyon area. Because Boynton Canyon is so large, you are less likely to be observed there by others.

I should probably also mention that some who have made love in the vortex have reported that it was spectacular—a merging of their energy on a spiritual level. If you and your partner decide to explore this potential in a spiritual place such as Boynton Canyon, I hope you will approach it as a spiritual experience rather than a lustful one. You are definitely dealing with spiritual forces and intense energy that you don't want amplified in the wrong way.

You may also wish to explore any psychic methodology you are already familiar with, such as the I Ching, Tarot cards, working with a pendulum, or automatic writing while in the vortex. I've personally experienced my most powerful response to automatic writing in the Airport Mesa Vortex. I've simply gone into an altered state of consciousness with a pencil and large notepad in my lap. I've then asked the spirits of the vortex to guide my hand and relate information that would be of interest or useful to me. Try it, even if you're not used to automatic writing. If you contact the vortex spirits, you will most likely contact American Indian entities. You can also call out to your own guides or highly evolved and loving entities who mean you well, to guide your hand.

Because of Bell Rock's beacon-like quality, it is excellent for attempting to contact higher forms of life, especially in automatic writing, as well as possible communication with extraterrestrials.

There are various ways to perceive subjective input while in an altered state. Once you have completed the body relaxation, the protection invocation and the countdown, I would suggest that you attempt to open for psychic input by asking for visions or conceptual input that would be of value for you to experience at this time. My own technique is very simple. I silently call out in my mind with the following invocation:

> Once more I call out to the positive powers of the universe, to my guides and Masters and those who share my energy. I am now open to receive positive information that will assist me in learning what I most need to know to evolve spiritually. I seek awareness as to my purpose and mission upon the earth plane. I seek your guidance and I seek a tranquil mind. I ask this, I beseech it and mark it and so it is.

Once you've completed the invocation, become very quiet inside. If any outside thoughts come into your mind, brush them aside and be open to visual impressions, your inner voices and your thoughts. Sometimes, the most valuable awareness will simply come in the form of your own thoughts ... which in reality may be directed by your guides. You may fall asleep and dream, which just might be what is most valuable for you at the time.

When you are ready to return to full beta consciousness, count yourself up from one to five and be sure to be very quiet upon opening your eyes. Have a pen and paper by your side or a tape recorder with blank tape so you can make written or verbal notes about what you have experienced. Psychic impressions and regression experiences are like dreams: they fade quickly away once you are fully awake. So make key notes immediately, and be sure to instruct others not to disturb you when you awaken until you speak to them.

It is also fascinating to attempt a past-life regression while in an altered state. Again, once you have completed the body relaxation, the protection invocation and the countdown, I would suggest that you then use an invocation similar to mine:

In the memory banks of my subconscious mind is a memory of everything I have ever experienced. Every thought, every action, every deed is recorded from this life I am now living and from all my past lives. I now desire to experience the memories and impressions of a past life that would be of value for me to explore at this time. I ask that you guide me and remain with me as I re-explore my own past. I ask it, I beseech it and I mark it ... and so it is.

Once this is completed, count slowly backward from five to one ... and be open for any visual or mental impressions that begin to come in. And be fully aware that you are your own guide. You can simply ask questions about what you are receiving to change the input or to seek greater awareness of that which you don't understand. When you are finished, count yourself up from one to five.

Now, let me give you a tip that may prove extremely valuable. Often when people are exploring in an altered state, they tend to "trip out." Tripping is usually a problem encountered by well-conditioned subjects. You don't go to sleep, but you trip away and do not remember anything upon awakening. There are several ways to solve it but the most effective is simply to verbally relate everything you are experiencing. This will not bring you out of trance. In fact, when I'm hypnotizing and regressing a subject, I ask them to verbalize their perceptions. By speaking aloud, you keep yourself from drifting off, and it may allow your partner to ask you questions. You can certainly try this as an experiment as long as you are inducing your own altered state. Please don't allow anyone but a trained hypnotist to hypnotize you. Although chances are that nothing negative will happen, with deep-level subjects, situations can occur that would panic an amateur while a trained hypnotist would handle it easily. If you're inducing your own trance, you can also easily awaken yourself if you don't like what you are receiving.

Once you have completed the body relaxation, the protective invocation and the countdown, you can use an altered state of consciousness to tap the energies of the vortexes for healing, or send the healing energies to someone you know who is in need. Or you can visualize the person you desire to see healed, sending the healing energy to them to use as they see fit.

Here is an incantation I like to use:

I call out to the positive powers of the universe, to my guides and Masters and those who share my energy. I ask your assistance in healing my physical body and mind. I ask that you combine your energy with the energy of this vortex to heal me now. I am open to

healing ... I am healing ... I am healed. I ask it,
I beseech it and I mark it ... and so it is.

Now, in your mind, draw down the light from above—
the universal life energy, the healing energy—and see it
as an iridescent, shimmering blue light. Feel the light
filling your body to overflowing with the healing power.
Make this fantasy very, very vivid. Then imagine the
healing energy emitting from the ground. Feel it combining with the light from above and then begin to
imagine, very vividly, that you are healed. See yourself in
your mind as healed. And as you imagine this, chant a
mantra silently in your mind, or speak it out loud: "I am
healing. I am healed. I am healing. I am healed." Repeat it
over and over, and believe that you are healed. Continue
this for at least 20 minutes while imagining the healing is
taking place.

A variation of this technique is to direct the healing
energy into your hands until you actually feel them heat-
ing up. If you direct the energy properly, they will heat up,
and when they feel as though they are on fire, place them
upon the area of your body that you desire to have healed.
Or you can, at this time, place your hands on someone
else to heal them.

Now, I'm going to get more esoteric. I feel that it is
possible to generate even more energy and power by invoking positive ancient powers. And my choice is the pentagram or pentacle—the five-pointed star, a symbol of
ceremonial white magic.

The pentacle is the star of man. Five is the number of
man and the star has the meaning of five. The horizontal
line is upheld by the soul, or the Divine principle. This
number denotes change and versatility. It is man
reaching out through his five senses for experience. In
ancient scriptures, it often pertains to the senses or to the
planes of manifestation. And, the pentacle symbolizes

spirit and the positive forces struggling against the forces of darkness.

For centuries, magicians have used the pentacle as a seal to prevent evil spirits from entering. If the star is used right side up, it invokes the positive powers. If used upside down, it symbolizes the elements dominating and is the pentacle of black magic.

In the vortexes, some people prefer to work within a pentacle. You can draw it in the dirt, form the pentacle with stones or, as some prefer, use cornmeal to form the lines. Be sure to draw it with unbroken lines by making five connecting strokes.

Then stand, sit or lie within the pentacle, facing the single top point. If you plan to lie down, face the top point to the north and lie with your head also facing north. Make sure the pentacle is large enough to encompass your entire body. Remain within the pentacle during all your explorations.

Some who are into ritual or ceremonial magic will use the ancient incantations, but you'll have to conduct this study on your own. It requires considerable investigation and awareness before invoking such power. Obviously, there are hundreds of variations of the techniques I've discussed and I hope you'll experiment on your own.

I believe you now have the general information you need to explore the Sedona energy vortexes. I realize I have gone to great lengths in cautioning visitors to the vortexes about the hazards—environmental, spiritual, emotional and physical—and in stressing the spirituality of the area. It is because I truly believe Sedona is a special area, deserving our respect and consideration. Furthermore, I would like to see everyone have positive experiences while there, and by warning beforehand of the possible problems, I hope they will be avoided.

I always outline these possibilities to seminar participants, and they are also a part of my **Sedona, Arizona, Energy Vortexes** tape album. **Ki Danielson of Seattle, Washington,** must have thought I was being a bit overly concerned though, and wrote me this humorous, tongue-in-cheek note entitled "Love-on-the-Rocks":

Contemplating my first lustless encounter in the vortex, I ruminate on the hazards. Will I worry about what's in my sleeping bag, outside, or both? Should my boots be on or off and will it be okay not to be pointing north? What if the cheesecloth gets all wadded up and my quartz crystal goes askew from its third-eye position? Will the fact that my car is illegally parked affect performance? Will I be shot by the guard if I return by the wrong fire trail? Will the physical activity be exaggerated if it's the new moon? Is it okay to make love in the desert to a Scorpio born in the year of the Snake, and do I dare to ask, in all sincerity, 'Was it okay for you, too, honey?'"

On the other hand, I was chided by **Monica Parsley** of **Virginia Beach, Virginia,** for *not* mentioning a couple of other hazards. Said Monica, "Also, highly recommend that people bring hiking shoes or boots (cactus goes right through tennis shoes and it's impossible to avoid all of it) and leather gloves (saved my hands and aided in the steep maneuvering)."

MEDITATIONS

Meditations in an energy-enhanced area are always fulfilling and uplifting experiences. As a part of my **Sedona, Arizona, Energy Vortexes** tape album, I included several meditations for use in the vortexes. If you don't have a copy of the album, a copy of the scripts is included here. You can read them during meditation or make tapes of yourself reading the scripts aloud or voicing a meditation of your own.

Before beginning each meditation, follow the instructions for achieving an altered state of consciousness as described earlier, or use your own favorite technique. At the end of each meditation, count yourself up from five to one and say the words, "wide awake, wide awake."

Focusing Healing Vortex Energy Meditation
(Insert altered-state induction)

...and I am now completely relaxed and at ease, and I feel total peace surrounding me here in the vortex. And I call out to my own guides and Masters to join me here in this place of intense energy. I seek your assistance. I seek to walk the spiritual path and to expand my awareness... I seek the wisdom to rise above my karma, and I seek healing. I ask for Thy assistance in healing my body and mind. I ask that you combine your energy with the energy of this vortex to heal me now. I am open to healing!

And I now draw down the healing light from above and I draw up the intense healing energy of the vortex below. I perceive an iridescent, shimmering, blue light coming down from above and entering my body. This is the Universal life energy ... the healing energy ... the God energy ... and I now feel it filling my body to overflowing with the healing power.

Concentrate now. Totally concentrate upon combining the blue healing light from above, and the intense healing energy of the vortex below ... I remain totally focused upon increasing and expanding the healing energy. My own guides and Masters assist me in focusing and concentrating and increasing and expanding the healing energy that now pulses through my body with every beat of my heart.

Concentrate now ... concentrate ... concentrate ... concentrate on the healing light and energy ... concentrate ... I keep my mind focused totally upon the healing energy....

(Three minutes of silence.)

And the internal healing energy continues to expand and I am now going to begin to focus the energy in the palms of both my hands. I continue to concentrate upon combining the blue healing light from above and the intense energy of the vortex below. At the same time, I direct this intense energy into the palms of both my hands ... and, as I do, my hands become hotter and hotter ... and I will continue to focus the energy into my hands until they become so intensely hot that I can hardly stand it any longer ... I will then place my hands upon the portion of my body with the greatest need for healing.

(Repeat for four or five minutes): And the healing energy concentrates in the palms of my hands and my hands become hotter and hotter ... hotter and hotter. I am healing ... I am healed ... I am healing ... I am healed.

I once more place my hands upon my body and transfer the intense concentrated energy directly to the area where it is most needed ... and I am healing ... I am healed ... I am healing ... I am healed ... I am healing ... I am healed.

(One minute of silence)

And now, for a few moments, I will visualize my body as perfectly healthy and fully healed.

(Three minutes of silence)

And I have just perceived my own reality. From this moment on, I experience a physically healthy reality ... I am healed.

And from this moment on, I am connected on a superconscious level of mind with this vortex. I can always draw upon this spiritual healing energy no matter where I am in the world. The connection is made and it is complete.

It is now time to return to the manifest world, and the physical beauty of the vortex. And I thank you, my guides and Masters, for your assistance, your sharing and your love. From this moment on, whenever I feel any form of negativity, anxiety or fear, I will sense your gentle presence. And I will respond to the situation as you would respond—with love, a tranquil mind and a compassionate heart.

(Awakening)

Focusing Vortex Crystal Energy Meditation
(Insert altered-state induction)

And I am now holding a quartz crystal in my hand... and I am completely relaxed and at ease and I feel total peace surrounding me here in the vortex. And I'm now going to take a few moments to concentrate upon the intense energy that is emitting from the ground beneath me. I feel the energy ... I absorb the energy ... I am physically and mentally charged by the energy.

(One minute of silence)

And I perceive the energy on every level of my body and mind... and I now call out to my own guides and Masters to join me here in this place of intense energy. I seek your assistance. I seek to walk the spiritual path and I seek the wisdom to rise above my karma.

I now choose to combine my own energy with that of the vortex and with that of my guides and Masters. I now focus this intense combination of energy into my crystal, concentrating the energy into the crystal... concentrating the energy into the crystal ... and I can feel it expanding ... pulsating and expanding....

Crystals focus energy and amplify body energy and thoughts ... and my crystal also amplifies the energy of the vortex ... and it is increasing and expanding ... charging ... and I can now feel the energy pulsation ... pulsing ... pulsing ... intensifying and building ... and for a few moments I will totally concentrate upon the combination of energy generating within the crystal.

(Two minutes of silence)

And I now quiet my mind and open to the messages that I shall receive through the vibrations of the crystal. I will remain in silence, open to insight and guidance. I feel divine presence ... I sense the light ... I feel the love.

(Several minutes of silence)

(Awakening)

Calling In Vortex Spirits Meditation

(Insert altered-state induction)

And the essence of the energy vortex engulfs me. I feel completely relaxed and at ease ... surrounded by total peace, balance and harmony. And I'm now going to take a few moments to concentrate upon the intense energy that is emitting from the ground beneath me. I feel the energy ... I absorb the energy ... I am physically and mentally charged by the energy.

(One minute of silence)

And I perceive the energy on every level of my body and mind ... and I now call out to my own guides and Masters to join me here in this place of intense energy. I seek your assistance. I seek to walk the spiritual path and expand my awareness ... and I seek the wisdom to rise above my karma. I now choose to combine my own energy with that of the vortex ... and with that of my guides and Masters, and I seek communication with the spirits of this vortex. I can sense your presence ... I can feel your intensity ... and I desire to communicate directly with you at this time.

I will remain in silence ... open to insight and communication from any positive spirit that remains here in this vortex environment. I await your communication and once I feel it, I will send out my thoughts and questions in the silent language ... and I will await your

101

response ... which I will perceive as an internal thought or visual impression.

And I am open now ... I await you with loving anticipation. ...

(Several minutes of silence)

And it is now time to return to the manifest world and the physical beauty of this vortex. I thank the spirits of the vortex and I thank my guides and Masters for your assistance, your sharing and love. From this moment on, whenever I feel any form of negativity, anxiety or fear, I will sense your gentle presence ... and I will respond to the situation as you would respond, with love and compassion ... and with a tranquil mind.

(Awakening)

Testing Unseen Energy Meditation

(Insert altered-state induction)

And I am now completely relaxed and at ease and I feel total peace surrounding me here in the vortex. And I call out to my own guides and Masters to join me here in this place of intense energy. I seek your assistance. I seek to walk the spiritual path to expand my awareness ... and I seek the wisdom to rise above my karma.

My immediate desire is to test the energy of this environment I now find myself within. I now open to all impressions and visualizations ... and the first and second fingers on my right hand will serve as initial indicators. Through sensory input from my higher mind and my guides and Masters, I will be able to feel answers in my fingers. I will always be able to sense more intense sensations in one finger or the other. If I feel any sensations in my first, or index finger, I am perceiving positive energy ... or an affirmative, yes answer to my inner question. If I feel sensations in my second finger, I am perceiving negative energy ... or a negative answer to my internal question.

So now to begin ... I'm going to take a few moments to concentrate upon the intense energy of this environment. I feel the energy ... I absorb the energy ... and I now test the energy.

(One minute of silence)

And I now seek to know more about this environment, so I open to visions, impressions, or I may choose to ask subjective questions and perceive the response in my fingers. I ask God, and my guides and Masters to be with me now as I explore that which is unseen to me.

(Several minutes of silence)

(Awakening)

Chapter Nine
More Vortex Experiences

As I mentioned before, the Sedona vortex experiences I am relating in this book represent three years' worth of research and hundreds of reports from **Psychic Seminar** participants and others who have written regarding their encounters with vortex energy. However, even people who have never heard of the vortexes have also had unusual experiences in Sedona. Sometimes, after they find out about the Sedona vortexes, they write me about what happened to them. Typical of letters I have received from those **unfamiliar** with Sedona's special energy is the following from **James Prater** of **Studio City, California:**

"I am registered for your seminar in Sedona, Arizona. I would like to explain why.

"About five years ago, I was hypnotized and asked to describe a place. I described the Sedona area in detail. I was asked where the place I described was located, but I did not know as I had never seen Sedona before. About two-and-a-half years ago, I arrived in Sedona to discover it was the place I had described under hypnosis. I returned to Sedona several times during the next year or so; and then, about a year ago, I had two very unusual experiences. The first occurred one day while hiking off the highway to Flagstaff. I was alone as I became very emotional—laughing and crying at the same time for no apparent reason. That went on for approximately 15 minutes as I was coming down the mountain. I didn't understand anything about what had happened, except it seemed to be some type of spiritual experience.

"I returned to Sedona a few weeks later and was driving up the highway toward Flagstaff just outside Sedona when I became very emotional again. That subsided, and I was a bit confused until I realized as I was later returning to Sedona that the same things happened as I approached a certain location. Then it dawned on me that it was the same area where I had the intense experience weeks earlier.

"I related these experiences to several friends, and they made statements like, 'It must have been the altitude.'

"Then I received the information in the *Self-Help Update* on Sedona. As I read your article, I could hardly believe the statements made by participants in your seminar. They were so similar to what I had experienced. The big difference was that I had no knowledge of the vortex at Sedona!"

Unfortunately, after the publication of this book, it will be increasingly difficult to find those who have not read or heard about these unusual occurrences. It will therefore be more difficult to ascertain whether the experiences related by those visiting Sedona are affected by things they have previously read or been told about the area. And, in a way, this is what makes the experiences related here even more unique. They have come from people all over the country who attended different seminars and never met or spoke with most of the other people who wrote to us, and yet, time after time, we see similar patterns emerging in the experiences related.

Don't be concerned, however, that reading these experiences will affect your imagination or your own experiences. I am speaking strictly from the point of view of an objective researcher. As such, I never have any way of really knowing whether what someone reports is a real experience or a fabrication, although my experiences and those of my family and close friends seem to bear out the truth of these reports. You, however, will "know" when you experience things in meditation, regression or self-hypnosis. You will be able to tell if it is real or not. Some of the most powerful regressions I have ever had all seemed as though I were "just making it up" and yet, the information I gained through these experiences was usually accurate and verifiable and always related to my present life. So trust yourself and what you perceive, and you will be able to relate its validity for your own personal situation.

There's nothing wrong with having a little healthy skepticism either. One should approach all spiritual experiences with an open mind. As I warned earlier, spirits can be lower as well as higher vibrations, and it's a good idea to use good common sense in evaluating your experiences. Obviously, there are things that happen to us that we can never explain, but as I said, if something real happens to you, you will "know" it.

Martha K. Williams' report is an example:

"I made this trip purely for the seminar—not the vortex stuff. Frankly, I didn't believe in it. However, the moment I arrived in Sedona, I felt it. I felt there was bad in the energy as well as good—whatever you brought here (positive or negative) would be enhanced. At the seminar, of course, I heard this was true. I thoroughly enjoyed every aspect of the seminar and feel the block I had been having has been removed. I am now a believer in the vortexes."

HEALING

Probably the experience easiest for most people to accept is physical healing. You have a pain, a wound or abnormal condition ... and it disappears. If medical tests concur with the manifestation of a cure, it moves the healing experience out of the realm of the "imagination"

107

and into the world of accepted "reality." Physical healings seem to be a common occurrence among visitors to the vortexes, according to the reports we have on file.

One particularly interesting case was that of **Nancy Hughes** of **Mesa, Arizona**. She experienced a healing from the healing circle at her first **Psychic Seminar**.

Then, about a year later, she had another surprise. These are the two reports we received from Nancy, in the order received:

"It was the first time I had ever been in a prayer circle. When you said to ask for self-healing or put in a friend, I put in my feet. I had a slight growth problem on the sides of each foot. Of course, after the circle ended, I checked out my feet. They were still the same, and I thought, 'Oh, well, it was worth a shot.' Then about four weeks later, I had my feet propped up on the coffee table and noticed something different about them. I examined them and was totally amazed—my feet were normal! There was and is no growth problem, and I have very proudly worn sandals the rest of the summer."

And the latest:

"Nine years ago, the doctors told me I was sterile. I was divorced and had two sons at the time, so I wasn't upset. In fact, the thought of not worrying about birth control put a smile on my face. I went through the healing circle in Sedona and six months later in Scottsdale. The Sedona healing circle really did a beautiful job of healing my feet. I never dreamed it would also put my female plumbing back in order. I'm now pregnant.

"Richard, I really think you ought to put in a word of warning to all your female participants in the seminars. Oh, yes, the doctor did a sonogram test today. I was amazed to watch my baby moving ... right into his brother. Yes, I'm having twins. Thank God I didn't go through three healing circles."

I hope you all consider yourselves duly warned.

The following are the words of others who claim to have received healing in the vortexes:

"Five doctors had advised me that the stress of several vexing personal problems was literally killing me. I went to the Sedona **Psychic Seminar** to try to rid myself of the results of stress and 'empty myself out,' so to speak, then recharge myself and my life with energy from the vortex. Many **great** things did occur, but only after the healing circle. Bell Rock sent me soaring in meditation and I received the 'breakthrough' I went to Sedona for. Since then, I am experiencing great things of all sorts almost daily. My health is vastly improved and I feel great. People say I look years younger."

Leo Shuler
Perryton, Texas

"The two guides who had appeared to me on the black screen in the clairvoyant session the night before, appeared not as a vision, but in voice only. They identified themselves when I went to the vortex. I wasn't expecting a lot, but I knew I'd receive all that I had come for at this time. I was instructed to walk along a dry wash, which I did, until I felt I was in the right place. This was a huge rock which was shaped like the palm of the left hand. I stood on the rock and raised my arms upward and immediately felt a warm, vibrating feeling on my hands. I was told, 'Heal thyself,' and was instructed to squeeze the poisons from the back of my leg above the knee, where I have a lump about the size of a cherry tomato. I was then led to walk in the wash as it had been cleansed by flowing water. As my body was being filled with energy, the feeling of being very light-headed gradually disappeared and I knew when my body was 'back in balance.' When I left the vortex, all that was left of the lump was a small lump about as big as the tip of my smallest finger, and by Sunday, it was gone entirely."

Anna R. Weisbrud

"I received healing for the torn muscles in my back when I went to Bell Rock. I had torn the muscles in my back two weeks prior to the seminar. I knew I couldn't do any climbing but I felt I would receive at least some benefits. I sat with my back against the rock base for quite a long time facing the sun. I felt warmed clear through. When I rose to leave, I looked back at Bell Rock and saw a very old man (I felt he was the high priest of all the high priests) suspended in front of Bell Rock, very high up. He didn't say anything, he just looked at me. He was dressed in a grayish-white robe, and I felt I knew him. I felt he was trying to help me remember. Later in the seminar, we did a regression and during this, I experienced more about the priest."

Maxine Parker
Escondido, California

"Bell Rock Vortex both times was a healing point for me. Both times, my hands became extremely hot and I asked for healing powers to intensify, and it seems they have. Airport Mesa last year was too intense for me. I could not handle it physically. However, this year, it was very different, although I felt like I was falling over forward. Boynton Canyon was freeing, calming and soothing, which is what I need in my life."

Sharon Hansford
Lompoc, California

"I could feel and see the healing energy flowing into my body while I was at Bell Rock Vortex, both in and out of the altered state. While at the Airport Mesa Vortex, I did a self-healing on a back injury I suffered over a year ago. I still have no pain."

Patricia Adkiss
Council Bluffs, Iowa

"During the healing circle, I felt the Kundalini energies zinging up and down the entire length of my body."

Name Withheld

"Thank you for conducting the 'Healing Circle' at the Sedona **Psychic Seminar.** My mom, who has had spinal arthritis all her life, has been in a lot of pain lately. She's had to walk with a cane, and hasn't been doing very much. Well, from the circle, I sent her the healing power as you directed. She reports that she hasn't been using the cane since Sunday evening (the time we did the healing circle). She also says she's feeling better than she has in years."

Helen C. Fredericks
Alhambra, California

"I received some answers to personal questions; also feel I received a healing both physically and spiritually. The vibrations at Courthouse Rock were very strong, but also loving and peaceful. I feel I received all I came for."

Name Withheld

"On the way out of Boynton Canyon, I banged my left knee pretty hard on a rock. I know that it hurt like mad, but after the healing circle, the pain disappeared **completely.**"

Name Withheld
Burbank, California

"We visited the Boynton Canyon Vortex Sunday afternoon after the final session of the seminar. We played the Crystal Cave tape along with one of your vortex tapes. During deep meditation, two of us were aware of the visitation of Indian spirits—seeming to look us over and giving their approval.

"I was shown a portion of the cells of my body—the 'space' areas were shining with white light. I felt as if I had experienced a deep purification and healing of my entire body."

Name Withheld
Fresno, California

ENERGY

One thing everyone who visits Sedona agrees on is the tremendous energy of the area and the extraordinary effects it has on people. Many report feelings of euphoria or contentment, and a common result is that most seem to need less sleep, food and liquids during their stay. Increased physical stamina was another experience, and some even found that the energy sometimes seemed to transfer into inanimate objects, especially metallic ones. Those who live in Sedona eventually seem to attune to the energy so that they are able to "normalize" their behavior.

These are just some of the many reactions to the energy of Sedona and the vortex areas:

"My most interesting vortex experience was simply the incredible energy I felt, especially from Bell Rock. It was such a natural high! The whole area induces euphoria; you feel as though you don't have a care in the world! We returned again to Boynton Canyon and Bell Rock on Monday. They are such addicting places—we feel an increasingly strong attraction to the vortexes. I'm in California right now but I just want to be meditating in

Boynton Canyon. It is such a letdown to be away from Sedona. I've never felt so drawn or seduced by an area."

Jeni Lyne Martinez

"I have never hiked in my life and after 12 miles felt like I'd walked a city block! The Airport Vortex is the only one that didn't seem to faze me at all. The other two were about as strong as the islands of Kauai, Maui and Kona in Hawaii."

Emma Gilliam
Alameda, California

"In the Boynton Canyon area, the energy level we experienced was unbelievable! After almost two hours of walking and exploring at high altitude, I felt no stress or strain. And, on top of that, I only averaged four hours of sleep a night and did not feel like I needed any more."

Richard L. Johnson
Dallas, Texas

"We find Sedona energetic and invigorating. We felt this on our very first trip to Arizona in 1978. We bought property at that time—Village of Oak Creek. We both feel more psychic here than we normally are.

"P.S. We made love in the vortex—it was wonderful!!"

Mr. and Mrs. Alfred R. Tanzi
Phoenix, Arizona

"On the first day, we went to Bell Rock. I weigh 320 pounds, so we didn't go very far 'up' to meditate (three steps up produced heavy breathing, legs trembling, sweat pouring off me, etc.). On the last day, we went back. It was strange—neither my wife nor I felt the least bit tired. I walked and climbed as though I were 18 again, instead of 46. We made it at least half-way up Bell Rock to the huge ledge that runs around the middle. Legs felt very young and springy, no out-of-breath panting, no perspiration. We both talked about it wonderingly. My wife made contact with an Indian, Jacob, both times."

Rodger K. Paulson
Oxnard, California

"At around 5PM, I went to Bell Rock, or rather, I was drawn to it from where the seminar was. When I got there, the feeling of relief was fantastic. My whole body was tingling with energy. Once I got out of my car and started walking, I couldn't stop. I felt as though 20 years had dropped off my 40-year-old frame, and I just kept going with no feeling of fatigue at all. By rights, at a 6,000-foot elevation, I should have been tired and stopped. I did huff and puff but no fatigue was felt. I couldn't get over the beauty of the area. It was as though I had been there before and I had finally gotten back and it was just soooo great to be **home!**"

John C. Harriman
Lynn, Massachusetts

"My wife and I went to the Airport Mesa Vortex. After the sun went down, it got chilly and the chill brought me out of an altered state. When I arose and began to write, my wedding ring immediately attracted my attention. It's gold with five diamonds, the center diamond being the largest. The ring was **glowing**, glaringly! I have never cleaned, though I had thought to do so about a week before the seminar. When my wife, Cynthia, came out of her trance state, I said nothing to her about the ring, waiting to see if she would notice it, too. And, although by now it was not as bright as it was when I first awakened, she noticed immediately. She said that you couldn't miss it! It was really extremely bright, and now **the ring has enlarged itself!**

"One more thing that is beyond our ability to understand: We're from Gresham, Oregon, and drove down in our '83 Honda Accord. Somehow, our car became electrified while in Sedona; the longer we stayed, the more charged up it became. By the time we left Sedona, the car was shocking us up to a distance of four inches away. The power lessened the farther we drove from Sedona. I'm glad because we were really getting tired of being electrocuted."

James Michael Morgan
Gresham, Oregon

"After the vortex experience, my life is totally changing. I knew it would as I was leaving ... and I've found that my outer and inner vision are both much improved. My eyes were totally clear and sparkling when I arrived home Tuesday night after driving straight through for 13 hours. Also, I brought home a couple of small pebbles from the Airport Mesa Vortex and put them in a plant that was almost dead. It is now healthy, green, happy and blooming. I brought another small stone to a friend, who immediately felt the energies from it. She was tired and down when I gave it to her; after an hour of holding the stone, she looked and felt totally different."

Dee Couch

"The few small stones I brought home with me from the vortex have a definite magnetic field around them. Several people have reported this. I know that, as agreed, I will have to return these stones to the place from which I took them. I tried laying them on my chakra centers this morning (all at the same time), and the 'boost' was powerful and most helpful.

"A professional psychic came within 20 feet of me and claimed to feel 'tremendous energy' coming from my body. She asked if she could hug me and afterward thanked me for it. She did not know where I had been at that time (later I told her)."

Irv Steinman
Corona, California

"From the moment we entered the vortex area, I felt an inexplicable euphoria overtake me. The feeling was akin to having consumed a few drinks without the negative effects of alcohol. After three hours of sleep, I had no trouble at all completing the 10-hour drive to my California home."

Name Withheld
Burbank, California

"I went to Boynton Canyon with several other girls I met at the seminar. I'm not very physically active and had noticed the high altitude of Sedona was causing me to be short of breath. In addition, I was carrying a 25-pound backpack as I walked the rather steep incline of Boynton Canyon. I felt sure I would be totally exhausted upon reaching a place to meditate but, instead, found myself so energized that I had difficulty reaching an alpha level."

Melissa L. Applegate
Clearwater, Florida

"I was full of energy before I even left for Sedona, but I certainly felt the special energy when I arrived. I also felt the difference after I left; it certainly was not present on Interstate 40! But I was so charged myself that I was able to drive back to Los Angeles with hardly any stops and without feeling tired! It really was a special experience."

R. H. W.
Woodland Hills, California

"In visiting the Boynton Canyon area, Bell Rock and Courthouse, I experienced the feeling of energy, but nothing else. I was on a constant energy high the whole time I was in Sedona. I also seemed to require less sleep but when I did, I continually had dreams I had dreamed when I was younger (approximately five to fifteen years of age)."

John Dansdill
Calistoga, California

"The vortex experience was awesome! I was feeling depressed and extremely tired as I drove to Boynton Canyon. As I neared the area, I suddenly felt euphoric and so full of energy I climbed nearly to the top of the main mountain in Boynton Canyon. I've felt utter peace and joy ever since! I feel totally in control of my own life now—confident, full of joy and completely energized! I'm fortunate to live so close, so I'll visit the area every month if I can."

Fran Madole
Prescott, Arizona

AURAS

Another phenomenon that seems to keep recurring in reports from the Sedona vortexes is the appearance of auras or "hazes" in the vortex areas and especially over Bell Rock and Courthouse (Cathedral) Rock. Since Bell Rock is supposedly a beacon vortex with energy emitting from the base and extending out the top for miles into the air, it is quite possible that especially sensitive individuals might actually be able to see the energy or "aura" of the rock. It is also interesting that most claim to see the color of the auras as blue:

"My partner and I had a wide range of experiences from seeing the pulsing energy around the Courthouse

117

Rock formation to experiencing a past life in the Boynton Canyon area and viewing the canyon as it was more than two hundred years ago."

Richard L. Johnson
Dallas, Texas

"I saw an iridescent blue-green aura over the hills. I focused and it went away. I unfocused and it returned. Also, the sky pulsated in patches of pale purple-yellow."

Frank Pollard
Detroit, Michigan

"I did get a feeling of the eternal patience of women from Cathedral Rock, and it had a lovely blue aura."

Tina Geoffrion
Auburn, New Hampshire

"At Bell Rock, about 2PM on a bright, sunny day, I was sitting at a point about half-way to the top. After trying to meditate, I began listening to one of the tapes and my sleepy eyes almost closed. Then, from the background of a nearby bush, I could see a fog or smoke-like substance moving rapidly up the slope. With eyes fully open, I could see nothing, but returning to a squint, it could be seen again. I thought there must be something here."

John T. Schurer
Denver, Colorado

"Sunday at dusk, my friend and I went out to Cathedral Rock. He put me into an altered state, and when I opened my eyes, I saw—with physical vision—one of the most amazing sights I've ever witnessed. The sky was still light enough to make out the clouds which seemed to emanate from the Cathedral Rock structure. Exactly when I opened my eyes, the entire sky was pulsating! It went from darker to lighter with the rhythms of a heartbeat. First the sky was bright, then it was shadowy. The sky and clouds were both affected. I have no doubt that I was witnessing with my physical eyes the energy heartbeat coming from Cathedral Rock. I was blown away!"

Name Withheld
Burbank, California

"I went to Boynton Canyon because of the balance. I found a very large, flat rock to lie down on. For some strange reason, I could not outline a pentagram, so I used a pyramid, using rocks for each of the corners, and lay down in the middle of it. My message was that I needed the energy and healing powers. After quite a while (I lost track of time), I was told to turn over, so I lay face down. I was told I could take the rocks I was using for the corners to make the pyramid after I returned home whenever my energy got low.

"The next day I went up Bell Rock. Aside from the energy I felt when I was leaning on it, I was delighted to see a beautiful turquoise aura around the top. When I closed my left eye and looked only with my right, the color immediately widened.

"I experienced visions of a beautiful blue crystal under Sedona. I had the feeling of a pyramid lying on its side. I have seen crystals in the window of an optometrist's shop with the same blue crystal."

Nellita Seabourne

"As my husband and I were leaving, I impulsively asked him to stop at Bell Rock. I took the binoculars to look again at the top. I examined it for perhaps a minute or two and saw nothing unusual. Suddenly, the entire top of the peak was surrounded by a deep purple, pulsing

119

aura. I didn't realize what could be wrong with the glasses, thinking it was some kind of reflection. I've never seen an aura before, but it finally dawned on me that that must be what it was. After awhile, it disappeared."

Adria Betty Elkins

"Airport Mesa: I went there by myself at dusk. I stood by the cliffs, looking at Bell Rock. I 'saw' white energy coming out of Bell Rock, but from its sides, not from the top. On the rocks to the left of Bell Rock, there was a strong blue haze; on the rocks to the right, a white haze. I had to unfocus my eyes to see it, but even so, this is not at all normal for me and I am sure I would not have seen it in broad daylight."

R. H. W.
Woodland Hills, California

"I initially 'tripped' for half an hour, which did relax me enough so that I was able to concentrate. As I opened my eyes while in my reclining position, I **literally** saw a dark blue light emanating from the sky, entering my head and my upturned palms. This is not my normal psychic *modus operandi*. I am very intuitive, but my visualizations have always been sketchy fragments against the darkness of my closed eyes. Still skeptical that this was only an optical adjustment to the bright sky, I moved my palms toward my body, then away from it. The light followed! My connection with God has always been strong, and His effect on my life profound, but this was more than I had ever expected from the vortex."

Allison Lane

SOUND

Bell Rock Vortex also seems to have another unusual quality—that of sound. Several individuals have reported hearing everything from bell tones and rumblings to beeps in the vicinity of the rock:

"At Bell Rock, I heard one high, sharp, bell-like sound. It was clear and beautiful."

Emma Gilliam
Alameda, California

"At the Bell Rock Vortex, there was this sound; it was similar to thunder, but it came from the Bell Rock, not the sky. It also was similar to a sonic boom, but not quite the same either. I'm not sure what it was, but, for me, it was very interesting to stand on Bell Rock, listening to this rumbly thunder that seemed to emanate from within the rock."

Name Withheld
Long Beach, California

"Bell Rock Vortex seemed to call to me in an inaudible voice. I was very drawn to it, and felt the energy from the highway as we were driving. Once we began climbing upon the rocks, I could feel their vibrations and could hear the rocks humming, almost like a generator hums. I also felt some sort of 'Star' or 'Interplanetary Connection' in this vortex."

Patricia Adkiss
Council Bluffs, Iowa

"I went to Bell Rock at dawn and planned to do my Tai Chi Chuan exercise with the sunrise. I had only done a few movements when I slowly collapsed to the ground. My legs gave out under me and I could barely move. I also heard a beeping sound from the mountain next to Bell Rock and then the same sound came from the top of Bell Rock. This beeping occurred about six times totally. I was told (automatic writing) that the formation next to Bell

Rock was hollow. I was also told that the reason I collapsed was because my body is unaccustomed to such energy and I 'short-circuited,' as one would say."

Diana Kruse
Aptos, California

Some have suggested that because this vortex is supposed to attract UFOs perhaps the sounds are in some way related. In fact, one seminar participant, an engineer who requested we only use his initials, said his wife actually claimed to see UFOs above Bell Rock. Although he wasn't able to see any UFOs himself, one of the photos he took at the time showed a strange spherical object above Bell Rock. The film lab could find no explanation for it. Here is his description of the encounter:

"Besides being the best organized and best run seminar my wife and I ever attended, it was the best preparation we could think of to experience Sedona and the vortex energies. For the six days that we were in Sedona, we experienced nonstop, round-the-clock psychic phenomena, each one better than the other. The experience I would like to relate is the physical manifestation of a UFO on film that we could not see physically, but appeared on a slide after it was developed.

"After arriving in Sedona and participating in the seminar, my wife and I noticed that we became extremely aware and sensitive to energies. We were attracted to the Bell Rock Vortex because of its known association with UFO sightings. My wife could see ships in the etheric above Bell Rock. I was frustrated because I couldn't see them, but had a feeling that if I took several photos of Bell Rock, maybe something might just turn up on the film. Besides, I am an engineer by profession and have always wanted physical proof I could show someone and verify concerning the 'paranormal.'

"Upon developing the approximately 180 slides I took on the trip, one slide had a purple spherical 'object' on it, directly above Bell Rock. There were no spots on any of the other slides. Some may say it's just a coincidence. The film lab confirmed that it was not a chemical spot on the slide. I know what it is!"

J. S.

PAST-LIFE REGRESSIONS

As with all other types of psychic energy experiments, exploring past lives through hypnotic regression seems to be enhanced by the energy of the vortexes. Many reported experiences similar to those of **Cheryl Bush:**

"I was able to see vivid pictures for the very first time. The experience was very exciting, yet frustrating, because putting it into words somehow isn't easy. It comes out so trite-sounding compared to the emotion involved. Also, in the regression experience, I saw things there is no way to explain. I've never seen anything in the world to compare to it."

Included here are a few of the past-life regressions encountered during the seminar sessions or in vortex meditations:

"During the past-life regression, I discovered the answer to a dream I had four years ago where I went through a death experience. The same death experience was in the past-life regression.

"In the regression, I was a young Indian girl in the Arizona territory in the 1870s, although I'm not sure it was called Arizona at that time. My tribe was quite small, and we were more or less farmers or cultivators, growing our own foods and medicinal herbs. We were very peaceful people, being more spiritual or metaphysical. I was apprenticed to a very old medicine man, training to become a medicine person.

"An older woman in the village was very jealous of me because the young man I was married to was the one she had wanted her daughter to marry. Also, she wanted her son to become the new medicine man, feeling it would give her greater power in the tribe as she was not well accepted by the others because of her evil ways.

"I remember being adept at many things under the medicine man's guidance, including astral projection. During one such projection, I was shown how to use 'star rocks'—quartz crystals—as one method of healing. Also, during this time, I was aware that this older woman was plotting my death, but could do little to prevent it.

"When I was about 19, my husband was killed in a raid on our village by a war party from a neighboring tribe. Later that year, our tribe prepared to move to our winter hunting grounds. I was standing near where the horses were tied when I saw the older woman coming toward me. She was very angry and full of hate. As she approached me, she picked up a long lance and stabbed me through the solar plexus area. As I lay dying, I left my body and looked down upon the scene. She was standing over my body, laughing. As I looked up, I saw the rest of the people riding away from our camp. I felt very sad because I felt I could have done so much for my people if I had not died.

"Then a glowing figure came and hovered beside me. I remember calling him the 'being of light.' He told me that this particular life had ended and I must go on to finish my purpose of healing elsewhere.

"My husband in that life is my youngest son in this life; my father in that life was also my father in this life; the woman who killed me is my ex-husband's present wife, bearing the same feelings of malice and hate for me.

"As a child in this life, I have felt fear and uneasiness around Indian people that I could not explain. Also, my father had a great yearning to move to Phoenix—that was all he ever talked about—but we couldn't afford to move from Montana to Arizona at that time. I have also felt this urgency to move to Arizona for about the past year and a half.

"I have been told by several psychics that I have been a healer in Atlantis, Lemuria, China, and Egypt, and several times I have been an Indian medicine person in the Arizona area. I assume that explains my 'Arizona Connection' and my inner feeling that I should move there.

"Strangely enough, I just completed a course in natural therapies. I wasn't sure at the time why I was taking this particular course, other than feeling the need to learn these techniques. Perhaps this is the first step on the road to my purpose in this life."

Patricia Adkiss
Council Bluffs, Iowa

"On Sunday morning, Shawndee and I were in bed in our room; I was relating to her my past-life regression of the night before which I had not yet written down. We were directed to relive the happiest, proudest day of that lifetime. I was telling Shawndee that I was so proud because I had been allowed to put up my beautiful, long, dark hair for my very first grown-up party. I wore a gorgeous red gown and a lovely lace mantilla in that life, and was so proud and happy.

"Suddenly, Toni, who was doing her after-shower things, getting ready for the seminar, burst into the room from the dressing area waving a paper, saying, 'Read this, Mom! Just read this!'

"The written account of **her** past-life regression was almost word-for-word what I had just been relating to Shawndee. None of us had discussed this after the session the evening before; we had simply gone to dinner and

125

talked of other things. It was just **one** of those amazing things we experienced. We don't quite understand that one, but it's still remarkable."

Shawn Mirich
Dolan Springs, Arizona

"At the Bell Rock Vortex, meditating on a past life, a vision appeared before my eyes: a brightly colored sun sign, bright yellow with spokes of gleaming white, seemed to embed itself on a rock wall. Leaning against the wall was a young Indian girl. She was in tears and very depressed. I asked in what way I could help—she seemed so alone.

"Weeping, she replied, 'I'm going to have a child and the brave cannot marry me. I am forced to leave my tribe and my people.'

"I asked her, 'Will you come with me and together we will raise the child?'

"As she came toward me, the vision lifted. I was then instructed to go back to Sedona where I was to purchase a certain item which I would be shown. I was to take it home to share with my daughter.

"Back in Sedona, I searched several shops and found nothing. Finally, as I entered another shop that sold mostly sand paintings, I was stumped. Sand paintings had never meant much to me, just a lot of Indian symbols which I knew nothing about. I began to go through them, one at a time. Suddenly, as I stared speechlessly, one nearly stuck to my hand. It was a Sun-God and Feathers. In the middle of the Sun was a small figure with many small, colored squares on either side of the figure. I didn't know the significance of the figures, I only knew that I had to purchase it. As I pulled out my wallet, I asked the proprietor of the store to explain its meaning to me. 'The small figure is the God of Fertility,' he said, 'and the colored squares represent the rainbow of hope and happiness.' As I listened, tears filled my eyes as well as my heart, only they were tears of happiness!!!

"Now I know the young Indian girl is my daughter now. I helped her through her life as the Indian girl and in this life she has gone through the hell of cancer with me that I might live. Ten years ago, I was told I had three to nine months to live. My daughter went to a special hospital where she learned to administer certain experimental treatments which she gave me for three years. Oh, it was pure hell. She has more than repaid the love I shared with her as the Indian maiden."

Norma Waller
Richmond, Missouri

AUTOMATIC WRITING

As I mentioned previously, one of the exercises people seem to find the most rewarding to do in the vortexes is automatic writing. Usually, during the **Psychic Seminar**, I or my co-trainer (one of a number of well-known psychics) will lead the group in an automatic writing meditation. We suggest that they contact a "wisdom entity," someone they admire who has passed over and would be capable of relating information that would assist the querist's progress, either spiritually, intellectually, physically or materially. This involves entering a relaxed state through meditation or self-hypnosis while sitting in a comfortble position with a notepad on your lap and a pen in hand. Once relaxed, the participants open their eye and allow their hands to write whatever comes. Often, if nothing is immediately forthcoming, it is helpful to keep drawing circles until letters begin to appear. It is not unusual for automatic writing to be different from your own handwriting, or even for it to change from time to time, as witnessed by a participant

127

from **Fresno, California**, who wished to remain anonymous: "The automatic writing brought surprises in that a new 'guide' was introduced about midway and the writing changed dramatically."

Entities contacted ranged from the "sublime to the ridiculous," as Napoleon once said. These are a few examples of automatic writings received:

"After making contact with a spirit in Boynton Canyon, I read some astrology charts with his interpretation. I placed my left hand over the chart and used my right hand for automatic writing. I would read what was being written, question where the information was in the chart, look at the chart and say to myself, 'Of course! How simple!' The energy was so intense, the feeling of love from this spirit so intense, that I was shaking and crying the entire time I was doing this. I received so much energy from there that I was up until 4 AM walking around with a flashlight at the Airport Mesa and Bell Rock vortexes. (I slept very well and awoke at 7:30 AM.)"

Name Withheld

"For a long time, I had visualized myself as sitting on a huge reservoir of creative power, unable to tap into it because of its stone shell. During my Boynton Canyon Vortex experience, two of my guides showed up, but I resisted them because they weren't what I expected. They were a couple of jokers—slapstick jokers. I felt a slight sinking feeling of disappointment. Dignified masters they were **not**. I finally decided to acknowledge them and find out if they really were meant for me. They told me they were my guides—for a while, anyway.

"One was a man with short gray hair and beard, rather professorish-looking. When I asked his name, he answered, 'Tamur,' readily enough. But the other character, manifested as a very odd-looking, slate-colored pyramid, just smiled and sniggered when I asked him what his name was. He and Tamur kept looking at each other, nudging each other and laughing. I couldn't believe it. Finally, he said, 'Just call me The Wedge.' 'The Wedge?' I asked, beginning to feel like a straight man. 'Yeah,' he giggled, not explaining. I was feeling somewhat bewildered by this time. I said, somewhat disappointedly,' 'You're not very serious.' 'Are you?' they responded. And I had to acknowledge I had gotten what I deserved.

"They settled down somewhat, and as they both looked intently at me, Tamur asked if I really wanted 'this.' Not really knowing what 'this' was, I still felt very definitely that **yes**, I wanted 'this.' Whereupon 'The Wedge' dove, headfirst, into my solar plexus. Surprised, but not alarmed, I asked Tamur, 'What's he doing? What's going on?' Tamur said, 'It's all right. He's cleansing some energies.'

"My solar plexus began to glow with an orange light— looking something like whirling molten lava edged with darker, harder crust. After a few minutes, 'The Wedge' withdrew. I came up then, feeling peaceful and content. I believe 'The Wedge' broke a hole in the stone shell covering my reservoir, which probably explains why I had such success in the automatic writing after that.

"Alan Vaughan advised us to contact a 'wisdom' entity, but having admired the immense talent of a man who had just passed over, I thought I would like to see what I could get from Orson Welles. I thought it might be a mistake, so soon (three days) after his death, but I figured he was an individual of some higher development and so I decided to try.

"After going down very well and calling Orson, I experienced a jolt in my solar plexus and my hand proceeded to write jerkily. I have never had such a decisive physical reaction before. I was and am very pleased. This is what I/Orson wrote: 'I want to be left alone. I don't want to be bothered now. Please let me be.' I sent him white light and love and asked to please learn something about how he died—I'm afraid I didn't want to let him go because I was thrilled with the contact. 'My heart failed. I have no more information.' I told him to feel free to come through me whenever he decided to manifest, and then sent him more peace and light.

"I decided to call someone I could depend on—Edgar Cayce. 'I'll help you, my dear. What would you like to know?' 'What can you tell me about myself?' I asked. 'You can begin a great work **now**,' he replied.

"Excited, I asked another question: 'Is there something you can tell me that will relate to all of us here?' He replied, 'Yes. I will say you have only to look to your heart's desire to find your spirit. I will come again, when you call.'

"I didn't know what else to ask, but I didn't want him to go. Edgar introduced me to an Oriental entity called Ma Jong, and then departed. The Oriental entity communicated, 'You will be a great inspiration to many. Do not fail them. Do what you have seen and follow your heart's desire. I will come also when asked. You are beginning. You must clarify your thoughts and shield yourself from the confusion of life.'

"An affirmation I received was 'I am a being of light and joy. I will be a channel of blessing.' And then Ma Jong concluded, 'We are finished.'

"I'm thrilled to pieces. This is the most physical manifestation of my psychic ability I've ever had. I can look at my pages of jerky writing as proof that I'm **not** imagining it; I'm **not** screwy—this is all **real**."

Carolyn Kuzma
Clarkston, Michigan

"Most important to me is discovering my capacity for automatic writing. I successfully did this on five occasions in Sedona and have continued at home with very interesting results. The attached message was received during the seminar exercise.

"As part of the experiment, I specifically asked to hear from this person: 'It was preordained that I would be here to give my life to free people from bondage. In one of my previous lives, I was Moses. My purpose has always been to free people from bondage.

"'I am going to walk in very soon into a body in Africa. We have spent enough time on apartheid. It is time for freedom for all nations. There will be a change in Russia as you know it—those people are in a different kind of bondage. They will start on a path of enlightenment. It will sweep the nation, there will be nothing the government can do to stop this movement. There will also be a tremendous change throughout the world. This will be very large in the third-world nations. The United States will be turned upside down with awareness.

"'You, Janice, are to write a manual of basic information that we will send to you, for all those people who need plain, simple language to explain the concept of love and the many dimensions of what you call God. It doesn't matter what you call him. The concept is real—we are all real and all part of God and each other. The peoples of the earth plane are finally reawakening to this remembrance. There are so many dimensions that you have forgotten but will now remember.

"'The curse on the earth is starting to lift. The many technologies that are so great in your eyes are only a preview of the many, many things you will remember and we will live again in Grace.'—A. Lincoln

"Falling into the category of things you 'just know': the many fast circles at the beginning and throughout the (automatic) writing is a channeling down of energy to a level which can be received by the physical body."

Janice Little
Cupertino, California

" 'This is for Marsha. Greetings to you, also of Lemurian stature, a wise one of old, readied once again — a kindred soul of once highest evolution. To you, Marcia, through Shirley, we tell you this! Our message to you is one of love in your recent endeavors of a very personal nature—one which Shirley is not consciously aware, but you know what is meant. You are one of the highest of the kindred and have always been so—respect yourself, your decision. You are once again on the path—your own path—do not be afraid. You have your own Masters and guides who love you and have been waiting a long time for you to open up! Be aware that we are kind, loving and will never hurt you. Now, as to your recent and present endeavors: Do it now! You know that you are ready. All you need is confidence. Have that and you are home free! Free ... free of thy self and into your truest nature. Remember always, you are loved by those above you and regarded in the kindest of lights. Always know this and forever seek, and you shall obtain! Farewell ... we will meet you again. You belong to the Beloved. That is all!'

"I have this funny peculiarity: whenever I hear or perceive 'truth,' I either get gooseflesh, chills and shaking, or I am moved to tears. The crying is spontaneous and can be very, very embarrassing occasionally. Anyway, Shirley got as far as 'Greetings to you, also of Lemurian stature ...' and I was bawling. What's really funny about this message is the 'waiting a long time for you to open up.' I grew up knowing that guides and Masters were around to help us, but I very stubbornly and

132

vehemently stated, over and over, that I would 'do it myself,' and 'I didn't need any help.' Only recently have I yielded to the idea of consciously seeking guidance and assistance through meditations. Capricorns can be so dense sometimes and, in early life at least, seem to thrive on taking the most difficult route possible. God, am I glad I'm growing out of that phase!

"So they really have been waiting. I have consciously and verbally pushed them away until now. Also, I have been vacillating over some decisions—three very major life changes. The message was accurate to my present needs and I did intuitively understand exactly what they were referring to as Shirley read the message. Also, Shirley got really choked up when she read the 'You are of the Beloved.' She said that when this came through her, she had the feeling of great honor, like this was a very wonderful and special distinction.

"Was the Beloved a concept of God? Love? An organization of kindred spirits? An individual? Poses some very interesting questions. Perhaps you could find out more from others. Also, was this a Lemurian term only, or is it a universally accepted word for a concept? I'd like to know.

"In the class exercises, I was able to demonstrate success in every exercise presented, which astounded me because I've never been interested in developing psychic ability. I am interested in further developing my ability to influence others to heal themselves. The energy of Sedona was attractive because I've recently been interested in the relationship of energy channeling in illness and chakras I only came for that reason. All this other stuff was a complete and unexpected surprise to me."

Marsha Lee

133

"As I was browsing through my favorite metaphysical bookstore, about a week before the seminar, I picked up a certain book, flipped through the pages, and put it down again, continuing to browse. For some reason, I came back again to that book and realized that I wanted it even though it was not the type of book I would ordinarily buy. I never had an inclination to read the book, but seemed to intuitively understand what was in it. I always kept the book on a nightstand in the bedroom where I do my trance work. What was even more unusual was that I packed that book to take to Sedona—2,600 miles away!

"I had just spent several years dealing with a medical condition that defied diagnosis. It was an exasperating experience, cost a hundred thousand dollars, and led me to the notion of writing a book to be used in medical schools concerning the improvement of doctor/patient communications.

"I had never participated in automatic writing prior to this time; however, I kept an open mind. As we were guided into trance, I chose the wise character of Albert Schweitzer, even though I did not know much about Dr. Schweitzer except that he was well-known for his medical work in Africa. I came to understand much more about this man.

"Dr. Schweitzer: 'Be sure to tell them to remember the patient is of most importance, to set aside personal feelings and concentrate their energies on that person. This method will bring much success and happiness to any doctor in the medical field.' I asked, 'Will you help me?' Dr. Schweitzer: 'Yes, I will be there to help you, just call on me.' Me: 'Is there any special preparation?' Dr. Schweitzer: 'No, just speak from your experience and from the heart.' Me: 'Will the book reach the right people?' Dr. Schweitzer: 'Yes, we on the other side will see that it does.' Me: 'May I begin soon?' Dr. Schweitzer: 'Yes, just as soon as you feel you are ready for the experience.' Me: 'Is there one quality that every doctor can use to treat **every** patient?' Dr. Schweitzer: 'Yes—love. It is so simple, but the hardest of chores for most men. Let your book center around this theme.' Me: 'Thank you, Albert.' Dr. Schweitzer: 'Best wishes to you. Tell Norman I'm OK.'

"As the conversation finished, it was as though Dr. Schweitzer and I became one spirit, blending with the universal energy. At that instant, an avalanche of knowledge was available to me. The seven-year medical situation was of a karmic nature with its purpose to bring me to where I am now: studying metaphysics, writing of the experience to lend a helping hand to advance those in the medical profession, and realizing my own unlimited capabilities. As trite as it may sound, I am not the same person who went to Sedona; I am on a new journey.

"By the way, the book I previously mentioned is entitled, **The Words of Albert Schweitzer,** selected by Norman Cousins."

Susan A. Matuszak
Granby, Connecticut

THE DOORWAY

I never cease to be fascinated by the similarities that appear in the reports on the vortexes. One particularly interesting situation involved four participants who claimed to see a doorway. Three of them were in the vortex at the same time but in different areas; the fourth was at another seminar. Here are three of the stories:

"Meditating at the left base of Bell Rock, my attention focused on the mountain to the right, just above the horizon, where I observed a small, bell-shaped peak protrusion. At this spot there appeared to be a doorway extending to the top of the universe.

135

"I was impressed: 'All is possible in the positive vortex energy. All one need do is find the spot and one can then enter the doorway, which is open to all; all who enter will go to the outer world and will be given eternal life.'

"After a while, I was instructed to bring a rock to my friend, Emma. Later, when I met her, I learned that she and another party had discovered a doorway just above the horizon of the mountain to the left of Bell Rock. I gave her the rock as instructed, whereupon she noticed its shape was the same as the doorway she and the other party had seen."

**Margaret P. Glatt
Oakland, California**

"At Bell Rock, I heard one high, sharp bell sound, clear and beautiful. Turning to the west, I visualized the vortex energy taking shape as a doorway. Margaret Glatt shared the above experiences with me; a man named Tony also saw the doorway."

**Emma Gilliam
Alameda, California**

"Spirits guided a friend and me to our special spot. He wanted to be near a river bed, but I wanted to be near the pine trees. We found a spot where the river bed ran over a large bed of rocks, like a short waterfall, by three pine trees. I did fantastic automatic writing and meditated. Upon finishing my meditation, I was guided to look up and there I saw a spirit on the mountain looking over us. He came through a doorway and looked at me. I felt an intense surge of energy. I came unglued at this sight, wondering if I were really here or in a dream. I asked permission to take a rock home. When I came out of trance and opened my eyes, there, on the ground next to me, was a perfectly shaped pyramid rock. I then asked the spirit if this was the rock, and he said to give it to my friend as a gift from me and them. (My friend is heavily into pyramids.) I was told to take a small round rock for myself and wear it. This was a great experience and a beautiful day. Thanks!"

Jacque Martinson

IMPRESSIONS

In addition to the different types of energy manifestations we have already recounted, many seminar participants wrote of various other impressions and occurrences that happened while they were in Sedona and the energy vortexes. These are a sampling:

"I came here to make contact with my ex-husband, who died one-and-a-half years ago. He was my soulmate. This was accomplished in Boynton Canyon with tears, anguish, then happiness for both of us. . . and release and understanding."

Name Withheld

"I've only done automatic writing once before in my life (at your seminar in Anaheim two years ago), and then only two lines. At Boynton Canyon, I received a full page of answers after a welcoming message. I found that holding my crystal over a vortex rock gives immediate and strong answers."

Tiena-Kay Halm

"On the way into Boynton Canyon, I received a thought. 'Take some rocks,' it said. 'Which ones?' I asked. The thought said, 'You'll know when you see them.' I walked for a while and then came upon four small rocks lined up side by side. I saw no other rocks lined up like that. When I picked them up, I knew that three of my friends could not get to the canyon; these rocks were for them. Later that afternoon, I met my friends and told them, before they could say anything, that I knew they couldn't make it to Boynton Canyon, and the spirits had told me to take some rocks for them. They were surprised and overwhelmed with joy when I gave them the rocks."

John C. Harriman
Lynn, Massachusetts

"When I asked permission to take a rock home, a voice spoke loud and clear: 'You already have one rock at home.' I left the rock."

Jack Hall
Valrico, Florida

"At Bell Rock, I climbed to a plateau where I sat in meditation. Leaning against the rock, I began to feel intense heat moving through my body. I felt several electric shocks go through my body. Then I **saw** inside the rock a platform with several colored lights around it. There was a large crystal at the base of the platform and, as the heat grew stronger, the crystal broke into several small fragments, dissipated and turned into rays of color. The waves of color then began to move toward the center of the platform and merged with the large crystal at its base. When this process was complete, I felt a tremendous sense of peace and well-being, my hearing became more acute and my perception more vivid."

Sayahda Viana
Douglas, Alaska

"I started getting pictures of the old civilization, then an inner voice said that this was not my purpose to see. My purpose was to restore my spirit and become one with the land and I would be renewed in energy and life. I felt the vibrations of the ground and a wonderful sense of peace. I wanted to cry out of sheer happiness. I left the vortex feeling touched and changed."

Jan L. Long

"I was able to reopen my automatic writing abilities in a much clearer manner. I received immediate answers to my questions; it was like a loving reunion surrounded by all my guides. I also had the experience of seeing a fantastic aura of one of the people accompanying me.

"The evening before, with the clairvoyant session, I had visions of a person fitting her body into a large rock formation that cradled her while she had experiences. I thought the session was ineffective for me because it had no meaning. Then, the next day, a woman who went to the vortex alone came back describing her 'happenings.' It was exactly what I had perceived in the session the night before."

Sonia Levy

"I felt drawn only to the Courthouse Rock Vortex. Of my first visit, I only remember coming out of trance with my face and neck wet ... apparently, I'd had quite a good cry but don't remember crying. On the second visit, I experienced a very rapid heartbeat and a great sensation of my entire body pulsing while I received the following affirmation: 'Joy is the essence of my being. It illuminates all I see. I am open to all healing powers, inner visions and perfect sight. I am complete, I am perfect and whole. I am indeed one with all.'"

Judith Brown

"Forming an arc between ourselves and another in the group that we wanted to meet, I imagined a light between

139

myself and someone who I had not been able to meet all weekend. He immediately came from across the room to be my partner for the next exercise. Maybe I should write a book on 'how to meet men'!?!"

Monica Parsley
Virginia Beach, Virginia

And so the visions, the past-life memories, the meditative insights, the healings and the energy continue. We could probably provide an endless supply of reports of vortex experiences, but that's not the idea. The idea is to make people aware that these things do exist and we can experience them for ourselves. Your own experiences in the Sedona energy vortexes would surpass any that you've read here because that experience would be unique; it would have meaning for you alone. When we seek to develop our psychic talents, what we are doing is seeking to improve ourselves, our relationships and the quality of our lives in all aspects.

Hopefully, all who read this book will someday get a chance to actually visit Sedona and experience the magnificent energy for themselves. But, if not, realize that all the experiments and experiences you've read about here can also be manifested in your own home. A trip to Sedona isn't necessary before you try automatic writing, past-life regressions, hypnosis programming or meditation. Don't use the lack of vortex energy as an excuse not to develop your own psychic abilities.

Chapter Ten
What Happens
At A Psychic Seminar?

As a little background, you might want to know what happens at a Sedona **Psychic Seminar** — individuals' reactions to it and how it seems to act as a catalyst for the myriad experiences reported in this book.

The seminar is structured for personal psychic experiences and development in such areas as telepathy, trance channeling, clairvoyance, psycometry, automatic writing, remote viewing and psychokinesis. It also includes past-life regressions and much more. Well-known psychics and metaphysical practitioners usually co-train the seminars with me.

Since the Sedona area, particularly around the vortexes, expands energy, including psychic energy, participants who have never experienced psychic input or ability have been absolutely amazed at what they could do psychically after the proper instructions and preparation. Once you have learned to test the vortex energy, then activate and expand it, the psychic potentials of your vortex experiences are greatly enhanced.

In our very first **Psychic Seminar** in May of 1984, 96 percent of the participants reported successful results in the psychic experimental sessions and in the energy vortex areas. After several **Psychic Seminars** with similar successes, I became convinced that we could take the actual training sessions a giant step further.

At the next **Psychic Seminar**, with the energy of the area intensifying the participants' latent abilities, we conducted new and highly successful telepathy and clairvoyant experiments. As the seminar progressed, participants were assigned to do psychic readings on each other. The success rate was phenomenal, especially for the individuals conducting the readings who didn't realize the depths of their own psychic abilities.

Of the 253 people who attended, only 21 were professionally involved in some form of metaphysical practice. According to the Advance Information Sheets, 80 percent rated themselves as having "no psychic ability, but I want to develop it"or "a little psychic ability." Almost every state in the country was represented, plus two foreign countries. The average participant had two or three years of college and many had professional degrees. At the end of the seminar, we passed out follow-up sheets. One of the things asked on the follow-up was, "Please relate your most interesting vortex experience."

Typical of the comments I received were:

"Since I wasn't sure what to expect and was very skeptical, I tried to focus on keeping an open mind. I was surprised at the success I had in most of the exercises and how well a person 'hit me on the head' with the 'fairy tale' exercise. I got in touch with a lot of issues inside me—whether it came from guides, higher power or whoever."

Name Withheld
Houston, Texas

"Thank you for validating my right to be psychic! I picked up the three symbols you sent to the group with an ease that excited me. (I also picked up the picture of a black and white dog during the transmission and wonder at this still.)"

Name Withheld
Burbank, California

[Editor's Note: Dick holds a Zener card—a card marked with a symbol, such as a circle, triangle, etc.—hidden from sight and concentrates on it while the group tries to pick up the symbol through ESP. Incidentally, a black and white Shih-tzu named Ninja is a member of the Sutphen family.]

"This is my second **Psychic Seminar** in Sedona; it's habit-forming. Because the environment and personalities are very comfortable, I was able to open up—my awareness has become so much keener. The psychometry exercise and reading each other were **very** successful for me. It is finally getting to the point where psychic ability feels 'natural,' somewhat like moving from kindergarten to grammar school, with a long way to go, but progress is quite evident!"

Sandy Tofflemire
Lawndale, California

"During the psychometry experiments, I was astounded when I gave my impressions to our little group. I really didn't know whose question was on the folded paper I held. I know I do automatic writing easily, but I didn't have much confidence with being able to give an accurate mini-reading on such short notice. However, when I finished, the girl on my right burst out that I had exactly expressed her innermost thoughts and desires, described her completely, and she was amazed because she had never had the nerve to admit these ambitions to anyone. I'd just gone with the 'words' that came to me."

Shawn Mirich
Dolan Springs, Arizona

"I suppose I was a bit skeptical at first and thought that I was making everything up. During the automatic writing session, the gentleman that I 'read for' told me that chances were one in a million that I could have zeroed in like I did. I have more confidence in my abilities now and will follow my intuition more often. This was truly an incredible experience."

Monica Parsley
Virginia Beach, Virginia

"The seminar was not only informative but showed me that psychic abilities are our right. I had believed that others had this 'talent,' but not me. The seminar showed me that I had a false belief; it is not only possible, but you really have to work hard not to use it."

Richard L. Johnson
Dallas, Texas

The usual flow of the seminar goes something like this: The participants are conditioned through altered-state and other sessions to perceive psychically, then are taught techniques to use in the seminar room and the vortexes. After a "vortex orientation" on Saturday in which I explain how to use the vortex energy and discuss the dangers involved, the participants are free to explore the four vortexes on their own. In the evenings, we often do past-life group regressions or use other altered-state techniques to explore and discuss the day's vortex experiences.

On Sunday, when psychic abilities are peaking, we conduct tests to allow participants to judge their own psychic accuracy. Most are amazed that they can do valid "readings" on strangers and receive information through automatic writing. Sunday afternoon covers psychometry and healing, often with incredible results. The Healing Circle meditation closes the seminar.

Participants frequently stay over for a few days after the seminar to continue their vortex experiences with heightened psychic abilities.

To give you a more intimate view: Shortly after the first **Psychic Seminar**, Sharon Boyd, managing editor of Valley of the Sun Publishing and co-editor of *Self-Help Update*, compiled information from participants for a report in *Self-Help Update*, Issue 21, entitled "The Voices of the Vortex." In it, she details events ranging from the participants' psychic experiences to threats of cars being towed away and encounters with a rattlesnake:

One of the most exciting seminars we've done recently was the **Psychic Seminar** in Sedona this past spring. Dick Sutphen, assisted by Alan Vaughan, guided over 100 participants during the fun-filled three-day seminar, exploring psychic potentials through a variety of awareness-expanding sessions, group exercises, experiments and hypnosis.

Sedona is a small town located approximately 100 miles from Pheonix. In the area is one of the legendary "power spots," or energy vortexes, mentioned in many different legends and tales from varying cultural backgrounds. There are said to be four of these energy power spots in the world; psychic and metaphysical impressions and experiences can be enhanced through contact with these psychometric areas.

One of the legends about the Sedona power spot is that it is the site of an ancient Lemurian city. During an outing to the vortex site, the group was asked to be especially sensitive to the vibrations and see if their impressions concurred with the legend.

Dick gave them specific instructions as well as a gentle post-hypnotic suggestion that any disturbance or background noise would only serve to deepen and enhance their altered state rather than distracting them. They were told to allow their minds to be open and receptive to the images, neither blocking them nor straining for them, but to just let the impressions flow and trust what they received.

The energy at the vortex was terrific; one woman confessed, several days after the seminar, that she was so charged up that everyone she touched was "shocked" and her electrostatic air cleaner would pop like crazy whenever she was around it.

All were excited by the adventure; several people agreed to let us print their experiences in *Self-Help Update* so our readers could share in the fantastic energy, too. Not everyone wrote their experiences and impressions down for us—some felt they needed time to sort out their impressions, others weren't sure they had received anything ... but those who did share with us had some experiences that were incredible.

A lot of Indians came through in the communication with the vortex; they indicated that the area was a very powerful energy area, revered and guarded by the Indians. There was also confirmation that a Lemurian city had once stood upon the spot.

Ray Calbert, from **Escondido, California,** had an interesting confirmation of the city; he meditated for contact with a leader of the time of Lemuria, and shared these impressions with us: "I was a Spirit Leader in the time of Lemuria. Many people question if it existed at all. I tell you it is an absolute fact!

"Many thousands of years ago, on this location, was the temple of the highest order of the Lemurian priesthood. For centuries after the demise of Lemuria, it was recognized as the source of the earth's power in this part of the world; each succeeding civilization has been led to recognize this fact.

"The Indians kept the area as Sacred Ground; only medicine men ever ventured near. Its significance has been known in recent years only by a few people, but the area is now coming into major importance once again.

"Lemuria was a lush and verdant country of tropical climate—fruit and all manner of vegetation grew in abundance and the people had the opportunity to become very spiritually advanced. This they chose to ignore; even so, their general advancement was far superior to that of most people today.

"They became embroiled in competition with the Atlanteans, as your present knowledge indicates. The quest was acquisition of land—a dream not yet purged from the minds of men even in your generation.

"They were extremely advanced in many ways—the printed word, medicine, and what you call psychic knowledge (teleportation, telepathy and precognition as well as healing) were ordinary occurrences in all households. Unfortunately, some abused these powers even as Russia is attempting to do today."

At this point, Ray's reverie was interrupted by the spectacle of a tow truck preparing to haul everyone's cars away. A cry went up from the crowd, and people began to run toward their cars. This was a disturbance that would definitely alter their state!

Alan Vaughan said that he was in communication with a long-time Indian guide when the Indian told him, "Go take care of it." Alan opened his eyes and saw a yellow Camaro being hoisted up in the air. As he started toward the tow truck, he heard his guide whisper once more, and the tow truck immediately let the car down.

During the seminar, Alan also channeled an entity he had never actually contacted before, but who had been described to him by three mediums ... sixteen years before! "Li Sung" made his appearance suddenly in response to a couple whom Alan had just met. "Li Sung" gave much past-life information concerning the couple and Alan, as well as giving other attendees valuable and interesting information about their past lives.

At one point, the flow of impressions and surging energy were so powerful and strong at the vortex that one woman burst spontaneously into song, channeling powerful inspiration from the ancient Lemurian vibrations.

Rebecca Betel, standing nearby, was so moved by the song that she asked why she was unable to unblock her throat so that she, too, could sing.

"I was in a self-induced hypnotic trance at the time," Rebecca said. "I started going back through my life, remembering incidents about singing. All the incidents that came up were concerned with my inability to sing.

"Finally, up came a picture of myself as a little girl of eight or nine, singing in a church choir. It was a fundamentalist Baptist church. The preacher's sermon was about how God punished sinners and which sins got the worst punishment. He finished by saying, 'Let us all sing a hymn to the greater glory of God.' At that point, the little girl who I was at the time said, 'I won't sing to a God who does that to people,' and I closed down and quit singing.

"I could physically feel my throat relax as I understood what had happened. When I opened my mouth to sing, I could feel how free my muscles had become. It was a wonderful experience of freedom for me." And Rebecca joined her voice to that of the woman, singing in beautiful harmony and wordless joy.

Rita Fincham received information during automatic writing concerning the ancient city and the song: "This area is holy and spiritual. There is an ancient city here. For your purpose, call it Lemuria. You are all citizens of Lemuria and have agreed to meet here regularly to maintain and increase the spirit of this place. Come back here if ever you doubt your strength. You were wise to come here to gain insight into your abilities. This is your ancient home and it is still here. The song you heard today was actually being sung in a temple in Lemuria; we wanted to share it with you in appreciation of your renewing the energy. The energy exchange is a two-way process—you give as you receive and we need your energy to continue. Believe in your power and it increases.

"Though hard for you to understand and believe, Lemuria is now and you are a part of both. Your collective mission is to share the love and wisdom so that it spreads. As it spreads, our power and abilities shall increase.

"Trust in yourselves and what you are doing. It is right and appropriate that you are all here at this time. We needed your energy and you have done well ... we are back on track...."

Robert Pelton, a calm, quiet man, related that he has always had a persistent, recurring fear of having people become dependent upon him. While raising his children, that fear became a constant source of conflict with his wife, Helen. He wanted the children to be able to fend for themselves as early as possible and his wife, rather naturally, thought that was not right. Her mothering instinct was offended by this "necessity" her husband deemed so important for the children to learn.

This fear even carried over to his business life; he had always tried to avoid the spotlight, preferring instead to work behind the scenes. Many people, aware of his talents, had tried to coax him into exercising his leadership abilities, but in vain. Robert said, "I know I can do this, but so far I'm not able to do this."

In the meditation regression that Sunday, Robert asked for the cause of his obsession. "I went back to a past life in Kauai, Hawaii, in the middle 1700s," Robert related. "I was a Kahuna, or priest, who had many people who were dependent on me for consultation and spiritual leadership.

150

"As my reputation grew, I became more arrogant and self-centered. Eventually, I lost contact with my God-self and began to feel invincible and omnipotent. I had become drunken with my power.

"When my advice was sought regarding an upcoming battle with King Kamehameha [*Note: Kamehameha was King from 1810 to 1819*] I believed my power would overcome the enemy. I advised against extensive preparations, believing, in my arrogance, that it really was unnecessary. I had been listened to for so many years that I began to listen to myself.

"In the battle, the entire village was slaughtered; I fled into the mountains, where I died a lonely death."

Realizing the cause of his fear will allow Robert to begin to apply his energies in ways that can be even more productive than before. "This has made me very much aware of the fine line between the use and abuse of power," Robert said after the seminar.

Not all of the inspiration dealt with the Lemurian city or answers to personal queries; one of the impressions received by **Art Mendez** was a beautiful message from an Indian guide: "The winds and the fire and sacred waters and Old Mother Earth have and know the power of the Universe, and, as unending as the wheel, play and replay the message over and over again, as the sons of sons before me have and as I have and as my sons of sons shall do—gathering at a power spot and recognizing the power of the universe, bending as the young saplings do when wearing the wind, we will

151

learn by the experience. But the giant oak that has been around a long time will stand staunch against the wind; it will break many times without learning the lesson. To live in harmony with the world you must learn to bend with your surroundings and love and respect all things as yourself; if you cannot, then the wheel will rotate—another time, another plane—and you will be required to learn the lesson again ... as it has been and how it shall be."

And so the long weekend flashed by; the eagerly awaited three days of psychic exploration seemed, when over, to have been all too brief.

One group, reluctant to end the experience, went back to the vortex site; they believed there was more they needed to discover. At the site, they began searching, moving rocks and pushing aside boulders. One particular area seemed to broadcast intense feelings to them; they were determined to push a large boulder aside, hoping to find a cave, perhaps, of the ancient ones.

Struggling and straining, they managed to move the huge rock.

"Ss-s-ss." With a flick of its tail, a small rattlesnake slithered out of the opening the boulder had concealed, and glared at the humans, as if in warning. A long moment passed, then the snake turned and vanished into the sands.

An omen, perhaps? Maybe the snake was a guardian ... then again, maybe not. A message **Lynn Sibley** received indicates there is yet much to be discovered in the vortex area:

"Wisdom from all ages, past and future, can be found here; remove blocks and anyone can find. Wisdom is available; this place is but one nugget in a whole strand of stones. It is man's choice to pick one place to let down barriers and give reverence and find solace. Magic is in the mind of the maker—when one has made magic one place, it is easier for others to follow."

And so ended an exciting weekend filled with adventure ... making and following magic.

About six months later, in *Self-Help Update*, Issue 23, Sharon Boyd did a follow-up report on the long-term effects of the vortex energy on the participants of the **Psychic Seminar**, with some interesting findings. In "The Vortex Revisited," Sharon explores the results of experiments with rocks taken from the vortexes and how the seminar affected people's lives:

What are the long-term effects of exposure to the psychometric influences of a large energy vortex? Does this energy impress itself upon the surrounding rocks, plants, water ... and can these effects be transferred to people?

We had already related the immediate results, incidents and impressions of the vortex experience in Issue 21 of *Self-Help Update*, and thought it would be interesting to see what the effects of the seminar were months later.

We devised and sent out a questionnaire to those who attended. The results were both impressive and exciting, underscoring confidence in the knowledge that we are all psychic. The **Psychic Seminar** stimulated new directions in transformational growth, resulting in intensified awareness for all who attended.

Reported increases in abilities already possessed as well as new abilities obtained through the exercises taught at the seminar included easier dream recall, greater healing ability, telepathy, precognition, automatic writing and channeling.

Approximately 83 percent of the respondents indicated that they already possessed some degree of psychic ability or had had psychic experiences prior to the seminar; almost 100 percent reported a greatly intensified awareness of abilities that—in several cases—they had not realized they possessed prior to attending.

Not surprisingly, the best results were obtained by those who regularly practiced the techniques they learned—ideally on a daily basis, though weekly practice yielded good results. Psychic abilities appear to be stimulated by regular usage, proving that, like many other learned abilities, practice makes—if not perfect—at least improved.

In about a quarter of the cases, new contacts were established at the vortex site, and were frequently continued after the seminar. **Maggie Le Page**, channeling Edgar Cayce through automatic writing, received this message concerning Dick Sutphen: "He is a warrior who is learning, but he is a good man. He has opened doors for many that no one else could ... he has done much good."

One of the most intriguing aspects of the seminar lay in the effect of material from the vortex on people and surroundings. The majority of the attendees removed nothing from the site, but many of those who did reported some amazing results. [*Please note: We are not encouraging wholesale destruction of the vortex site by irresponsible souvenir seekers, but we feel that a small stone, pebble, leaf or twig cannot affect the vast energy of the vortex if permission is first obtained from the vortex spirits.*]

Mary Anne Fritts told us, "I took two rocks from the spot where I felt the greatest energy. I keep the rocks in my kitchen; whenever I feel depression or stress, I hold one in each hand above my head in a 'star' position. Now, this sounds stupid, but when I do this, all the bad feelings are gone—period—just gone in a flash!" No, Mary Anne, this does not sound stupid. T. C. Lethbridge has written much about stone imprinting—the impression of energy upon rock—which have carried their psychometric charges throughout millennia. These effects are greatly magnified in areas around ley lines and energy vortexes, such as the one at Sedona, and have been written about by John Michell in **The View Over Atlantis** and **The New View Over Atlantis,** and J. Havelock Fidler in **Ley Lines.**

Nancy Hughes related the details of an interesting experiment she conducted: "I broke a couple of rocks up and put them around my plants. They doubled in growth in two weeks. I put some of them around plants that were nearly dead; they're healthy and huge now.... I found keeping the rocks in the sun keeps them active."

She also performed tests using the rocks with friends, one who suffered from severely debilitating migraines, the other from insomnia following painful back surgery. Nancy reported that her friend's migraines vanished within minutes after holding the rocks. A piece of rock under the pillow of the insomnia sufferer alleviated her sleeplessness and encouraged the back to heal in half the normal time following surgery.

Further testing revealed that vortex water—obtained by a process similar to that used to produce flower essences and gem elixirs—produced the same beneficial results as the actual vortex material itself. This indicates that the energy absorbed by an object in the vortex can be transferred to another medium easily, rather like charging a battery. Nancy is eagerly planning further testing of vortex materials' effects upon vegetable growth.

These effects are not limited to plant growth and pain alleviation: **Peter** and **Betty Baird** report a phenomenal increase in "good luck" affecting all aspects of their lives. "We took two small stones," they told us. "Our good luck, improved marriage, dramatically improved business and income make us wonder if there is a relationship. Who knows? But we sure wouldn't give up those two stones! During the past six months, our income has nearly doubled—in surprising, unpredictable ways." Of course, these results are not due exclusively to the effects of the Sedona stones; much of their "good luck" should be attributed to the increased awareness the seminar generated.

In **Judy Hall's** opinion, the most valuable result of the seminar was "the great sense of peace and oneness ... which the group generated. I think that together we magnified the potential of the vortex." Another woman stated, "I realized I could do a lot more psychically than I thought I could and I had been doing so long before the seminar."

April Tweddell's comment synthesized the general attitude toward the **Psychic Seminar:** "I understand and have complete faith in everyone's ability to use their psychic abilities. It is not merely a gift bestowed on a few. I accept and expect my life to flow psychically. When I ask the universe for something, I get it. The seminar has made me very clear about what I want and ask for. I feel a real unity with the universe now, a feeling I did not have before.... I feel very comfortable with the concept of death, or passing over to the spirit planes ... my life runs more smoothly and clearly. In general, I have a much deeper understanding of the nature of reality."

Laurence Hiscock commented, "At the time, I didn't think I got much from it, but now I am becoming more self-assured.... It's hard to explain ... my power of positive thinking is much stronger, beginning to come to me more and more."

Mary Anne Fritts enthused, "No experience could top the seminar! That was minute-by-minute amazement—hours crammed with one incredible happening after another. Upon returning home, I was eager to try out my new abilities on everyone." More seriously, she added, "That is, until I took a friend's hand to 'read' for her. I saw and felt only a terrible sadness that was hard to relate. Frankly, it scared me. I learned in that flash what a responsibility psychic ability is."

Indeed it is ... but used in a mature way by self-aware individuals, psychic ability and power enhance every aspect of life. A part of every human's nature, it can be ignored ... or developed and used, reaffirming the psychic nature inherent in every being in the universe.

One of the most recent surveys conducted at the **Psychic Seminar** contained only three questions:

1. What is your reaction to Sedona?

2. Do you feel more psychic here than you normally are?

3. What was your most interesting vortex experience?

Answers to the first question, although diverse, were always positive.

As to feeling more psychic, most people agreed that the vortex energy raises spiritual consciousness and psychic awareness. This was probably best expressed by **E. Kay Hood** of **Birmingham, Michigan,** who said she felt more psychic "because I'm surrounded by people possessing positive thinking and the desire to search for closer contact with higher consciousness/self," and **Jeanne Arnew** of **Prescott, Arizona,** who answered, "It's easier to achieve an altered state and to receive impressions."

We got a wide range of responses to the third question, including this one from a woman who had been given a "healing weight loss" while in the vortex:

Question 1: "Beautiful!"

Question 2: "Somewhat, but not dramatically. I trust my intuition all the time."

Question 3: "I went to Bell Rock with no particular expectation and started to sit down on a rock when a voice inside my head said, 'Okay, Aquarius, come sit by the water.' There was a small trickle of water coming down a nearby rock, so I sat beside it. Planning to use automatic writing as Dick instructed, in my notebook I wrote, 'Is it important for me to be here?' The answer was instantly in my mind ... very strong: 'Only for the healing.' This surprised me because I am very healthy, except for being about 50 pounds overweight. As that thought crossed my mind, another strong message came in: 'That is the healing!'

"I then felt some rumbling rumblings and unusual movement in my stomach and intestines. When I came down off the rock, everyone was talking about how hungry they were ... except me. My appetite seems to be cut in half. Whether or not this will last and be a 'cure' remains to be seen. I'll let you know."

Betty Chapman
Palm Springs, California

Betty did keep us informed. Four weeks after the seminar, she wrote to us, reporting a weight loss of 12 pounds. A month later, she had lost 20 pounds. The next letter, six weeks later, ecstatically told of a weight loss totaling 30 pounds and a new man in her life. And a mailgram, received two months after that, said, "Regret that prior commitments keep me from joining you in Sedona this time. I wanted to strut my new figure and wardrobe, as well as the handsome new man in my life. I have lost 35 pounds since the last Sedona seminar and have gone from a snug size 18 to a loose size 12. My whole life has changed, and it started in Sedona. I'll be there to

tell you all the details next time. Thanks a million!"—
Betty Chapman

Question 1: "This is the most beautiful, serene, psychic place I've ever been. Everyone and everything is just breathtaking!"

Question 2: "I came with my psychic ability really low, but I've been positively upbeat—really have 'tuned-up' psychically, which amazes me!"

Question 3: "While meditating, a beautiful Indian spirit came to me and I felt that he blessed my presence. I picked up a stone and asked the spirits if I could have it. I said, 'If you want me to have it, make it warm.' Nothing happened, so I dropped it and walked further along until I found another stone ... this time, it turned hot in my hand!"

Alouise V. Watson
Desert Hot Springs, California

Question 1: "High energy ... I do not need to eat as much or drink as many fluids here."

Question 2: "Yes! I normally do not experience 'seeing' color, pictures, etc., when I explore psychically."

Question 3: "I'd never tried automatic writing, but Dick convinced me to try it. My first attempt in Boynton Canyon resulted in writings I couldn't read. But when I opened my eyes, I saw a vivid vision. The colors were brilliant and the air seemed to be very thick and 'soupy.' I then received a special message from my own guide.

"As I explained to Dick during a break, I wanted very badly to come to this seminar, but didn't have the money. Not knowing how I'd get it, I put down the deposit to reserve my place. Two days later, one of seven tickets I was holding in the Colorado Lottery turned out to be a $500 winner.

"Upon my arrival in Sedona, I set about looking for a hotel, having made no reservations. I finally found what I was told was the last place in town which included a Saturday night reservation. The only room in town was #7, again my lucky number. Indeed, this has been an eye-opening experience!"

Rod Gillmine
Eagle, Colorado

Question 1: "I'm jealous of anyone fortunate enough to live here. It is such a vital, invigorating and beautiful place."

Question 2: "Yes, I really do! The instructions from Dick certainly help. I have seen great results."

Question 3: "In Boynton Canyon, I heard chanting like that on your music tape, 'Crystal Cave.' Then I saw an immense cavern with walls and ceiling of huge crystals. There were figures ... almost like mummies. They were still in meditation postures and were wearing dark brown robes. They had long gray and white hair."

Lois T. Leonard
Tucson, Arizona

Question 1: "I have experienced an extreme energy which causes tingling sensations on my brow, head area, and hands. The latter is really interesting because my hands are nerve damaged and I normally have no feeling in them at all."

Question 2: "Very definitely so, because I'm generally not psychic at all, but the last few days I've known what Dick, my roommate, and the TV were going to say before they said it."

Question 3: "At Boynton Canyon, when I went into meditation, a deep male voice said, 'Ru Ruid ... Ra

Rhuim.' I don't have the faintest idea what that means, but my purpose in this life became very clear to me. I was told I had cleared most of my karma, except for that with my ex-husband."

Rosalind Hanaway
Yucca Valley, California

Question 1: "Magnificent!"

Question 2: "Visions are more vivid and clearer."

Question 3: "In the vortex, I lay down with my head facing north and with a large crystal on my forehead and a small one on my solar plexus. I then began to meditate. First, a vivid emerald green, as if I'd stepped into a green overcast day. I was there and I looked down and saw my feet walking in moccasins and I was wearing fringed leather pants. Then I was running and I saw all the canyons and mesas as if I had lived in the area before. Everything was shaded in green but the views were superb.

"Then everything began to turn purple and violet, and I was running toward a man dressed as a medieval friar. He was half-turned to me, beckoning to me. I ran to him, but a dark mist flowed between us and I couldn't go any further. It was as though something were holding me back. I'm still trying to put this together with the many other experiences I had."

John C. Harriman
Lynn, Massachusetts

Question 1: "This is my third 'high' here! Love the energy and group communion."

Question 2: "Yes, since I'm a relative newcomer to metaphysics, I feel I have made great strides the past few days in getting my own self out of the way of my psychic abilities."

Question 3: "Intense vibrations in my body, particularly my hands."

Ruth Kemp
Carlsbad, California

Question 1: "It is a beautiful, peaceful place. I feel it is conducive to 'psychicness' for me only because I do not feel the need to protect or close myself off here."

Question 2: "No, I am normally quite empathic, and pick up emotions and physical feelings of others readily. I have random, uncontrolled experiences of knowing things. I work with dreams a lot."

Question 3: "In the Boynton Canyon area, I had a panicked "crowd" reaction. I felt surrounded by people—all talking to each other and to me at once. It was quite unpleasant. I felt the need to get away, out to wide open spaces. I found a spot where I was alone and sat for a while, but was distracted by a buzzing sound, like the murmur of a huge crowd in the next room.

"Objectively, I know I encountered four people in the hour and a half I was there. They were all quiet and friendly. I have had the panic reaction of feeling enclosed by others' energy repeatedly in the past, but I have always truly been in a crowded place.

"I have three theories: 1. My husband was panicking in a crowd and I picked it up empathically; 2. Many spirits in the area were successfully trying to get my attention and I was unable to focus on one; 3. It doesn't mean anything. I was just paranoid that day."

Kim March-Force
Benson, Arizona

Although the reports in this book are very representative of those experienced by the majority of responding seminar participants, all are subjective and, in most cases, different. It would be a mistake to come to Sedona with preconceived expectations. The area appears to be very spiritual and highly charged with energy, resulting in people being more empathic. However, I should point out that there is no guarantee of this.

It is also important to be aware that the Sedona energy seems to intensify your own personal energy, whether positive or negative, and the energy between people. Therefore, your state of being while in Sedona may very well determine how you experience it.

From all accounts, it seems to be a positive and worthwhile experience. The fact that the seminars are almost always filled to capacity (250 plus) even though we schedule them two or three times a year, and that many participants come back again and again, makes me feel that it continues to be a spiritual growth experience.

It is probably best expressed in the participants' own words:

"The seminar was one of the very best events of my life. It came at the end of a five-year period of very unsettling happenings in my life and I was at a point of confusion. The seminar melded all the good things I'd gleaned from the past five years, for I have been searching diligently. Everything came together in a clear, simple picture. The seminar was the beginning of my new life. It's almost a month later, and I'm still on my 'Sedona high.' Everything in my life is so much easier now—everything is changing or has changed, and I'm headed in a completely positive direction."

Name Withheld
Topeka, Kansas

"I spent a week, in addition to the seminar days, in Sedona. My overall energy increased to the extent that I took action on a work-related situation that had been a problem for years."

John T. Schurer
Denver, Colorado

"I thoroughly loved every minute I was there—loved all the people there, including myself (it's hardest sometimes to love one's self) unconditionally. I loved the energy and everything about all of it."

Dee Couch
Burley, Idaho

"Although I have been concentrating on working on spiritual development for some time now, I have had trouble visualizing and also difficulty trusting my 'mental impressions.' Gradually, I have improved with the trusting. During this seminar, I began visualizing more frequently and clearly, and also began being more accurate with information through impression."

Frank H. Small, III
Gaithersburg, Maryland

"I learned that I am a very deep-level hypnosis subject. I always thought before that I was simply falling asleep, since I could not consciously remember what happened upon coming out of the altered state. I still must learn not to go too deep while meditating."

Patricia Adkiss
Council Bluffs, Iowa

"It has taken me years to 'trust myself,' but I am beginning to. I believe the meaning of the seminar for me was to **listen**, and to become motivated to write the book I have been promising to write since the various guides began channeling through me. Why are we so hard to convince? There are so very few persons to whom I would even mention the writings, that it is a blessed relief to be part of a high-consciousness gathering such as you had in Sedona. We thank you also for being so down-to-earth about it all. We enjoyed your marvelous sense of humor and light-hearted yet serious approach to the different exercises."

Shawn Mirich
Dolan Springs, Arizona

"It brings together people who have trodden the path before. I knew I had to come. I was coming home."

Maxine Parker
Escondido, California

Chapter Eleven
A Preview?

On a July 1986 radio show, the host asked me, "Richard, exactly what do you think the Sedona vortexes amount to? How do you explain the experiences people have there?"

I responded by saying, "After years of exploring in Sedona, I think the vortexes can be summarized as an 'energy enhancing field.' In other words, the energy emitting from the vortexes intensifies an individual's own energy. So, if an individual is interested in tapping into his psychic energies, he will experience an enhancement of those energies while in Sedona. But if an individual comes to Sedona filled with negativity, then his negativity will also become intensified. The vortexes will affect all areas of your life, and even the energy between you and someone else. If your relationship is positive, it will probably become more positive while in the area. The same would be true in reverse.

"Is there some great crystal buried there? Maybe, but despite the evidence, I personally tend to doubt it. And if there is, what does it matter? Is Sedona on ley lines with other great spiritual areas? Sure, but so what? What is important is that your energy is enhanced when you are in the vortexes. Psychic energy, healing energy, love energy, and energy that can be used to go within and find your own answers may be a little easier in the vortexes than elsewhere.

"I don't see it as metaphysical or spiritual. The energy is just what is, and it can be explained in very down-to-earth terms. Albert Einstein discovered that matter is energy. A rock appears to be solid, but in reality it is a mass of vibrating, pulsating molecules. The same is true of plants, animals and people. We are all energy. Your body is energy. Your mind is energy. Your soul is energy. The only difference between them is the vibrational rate. It may be that when you enter the vortex areas, your vibrational rate is increased. Even a minimal increase in your vibrational rate would enable you to do things and experience things beyond your normal abilities. I contend we are all here on earth to evolve spiritually. As we evolve, we increase our vibrational rate. Maybe the Sedona vortexes provide us with a preview of our natural abilities a few lifetimes down the evolutionary road."

Bibliography

Barnett, Franklin. *Viola Jimulla: The Indian Chieftess.* Prescott, Arizona: Prescott Yavapai Indians, 1968.

Hodge, Hiram C. *1877 Arizona As It Was.* Glorieta, New Mexico: Rio Grande Press, Inc., 1965.

Khera, Sigrid. *The Yavapai of Fort McDowell.* Fountain Hills, Arizona: Fort McDowell Indian Community, 1978.

Schnebly, Ellsworth M. "How Sedona Was Named," *Those Early Days....* Sedona, Arizona: Sedona Westerners, 1975.

Thompson, Albert E. "The Story of Sedona," *Those Early Days ....* Sedona, Arizona: Sedona Westerners, 1975.

Yavapai-Prescott Tribe
Box 348
Prescott, Arizona 86302

Rio Grande Press, Inc.
Box 33
Glorieta, New Mexico 87535

Fort McDowell Indian Community
Box 17779
Fountain Hills, Arizona 85268

Those Early Days ... are available;
write for price information:
Sedona Public Library
Box 1507
Sedona, Arizona 86336

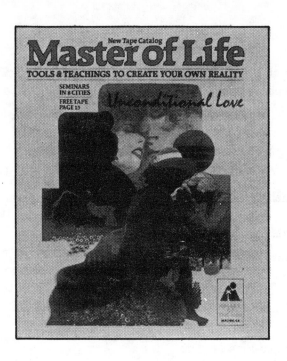

Write for a free copy of *Master of Life* magazine. It contains news and articles on the subjects of reincarnation, psychic exploration and self-help, in addition to complete information on all Sutphen Seminars and over 300 self-help and self-exploration tapes from Valley of the Sun Publishing: hypnosis, meditation, sleep programming, subliminal programming and New Age music.

Valley of the Sun Publishing
Box 3004, Agoura Hills, CA 91301
818/889-1575

Dick Sutphen is an author, trainer and innovative hypnotist who specializes in regression and reprogramming. He developed the group hypnosis exploration techniques that are now being used internationally. His bestselling books, **You Were Born Again To Be Together** and **Past Lives, Future Loves** have become classic metaphysical/self-help titles (Simon Schuster Pocket Books). **Unseen Influences**, his third book from Simon Schuster, was released in May, 1982.

Dick has appeared on many TV shows such as **The Phil Donahue Show** and **Good Morning America**. In 1976, he conducted the first nationally broadcast past-life regression on **Tom Snyder's NBC Tomorrow Show**. A 1¾-hour **David Susskind Show** was built around Dick's work and is still being rerun years later as one of the series' most popular programs. In the last six years, he has appeared on over 350 other radio or television shows. Articles about Dick and his work have appeared throughout the country in numerous local and national publications.

Dick is the author of 35 books and the founder and former director of a hypnosis center in Scottsdale, Arizona. He has an 18-year-background in psychic investigation and human-potential exploration. Today, he conducts his world-famous seminar trainings throughout the country. More than 55,000 people have attended a Sutphen Seminar.

Dick Sutphen lives with his wife, Tara, in Malibu, California. He continues to write, and he directs the activites of The Sutphen Corporation, Valley of the Sun Publishing and Reincarnationists, Inc., all located in nearby Agoura Hills, California.

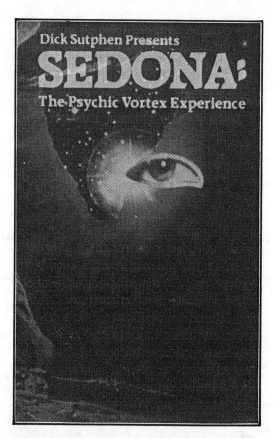

SEDONA: THE PSYCHIC VORTEX EXPERIENCE
By Dick Sutphen   **(Item BTA202 & VHS102)**   **$39.95**

If you enjoyed this book, **Sedona: Psychic Energy Vortexes**, we hope you'll be interested in the new video, **Sedona: The Psychic Vortex Experience.** For an hour, you will explore the vortexes with Dick Sutphen and some of his seminar participants. The incredibly beautiful scenery is combined with shots of people telling of their experiences and with special effects to simulate what has transpired.

Taped by a CBS-affiliate television documentary team from Phoenix, Arizona, and one of California's top computer graphics special effects artists, Denise Gallant. Available in VHS or BETA format for $39.95. Order from your dealer or directly from **Valley of the Sun Publishing, Box 38, Malibu, California 90265.** Please enclose $2.50 for postage and handling.

SEDONA, ARIZONA ENERGY VORTEXES

By Dick Sutphen (Item No. RA202) $45.00
4 Cassette Tapes (8 Programs) & Vortex Location Map

Everything you need to explore the vortex energy on your own in Sedona, or at home using the enclosed red rock we were given permission in meditation to take from the Boynton Canyon Vortex. While doing the meditation experiments, place the rock on your third eye, or psychic center acupressure point at the base of your chest bone. Sedona is probably the world's greatest "power spot," with more positive energy vortexes than any place on earth. The detailed map and Dick's instructions guide you to the exact location of the four primary vortexes.

Tapes 1 & 2: SEDONA ENERGY VORTEXES—Dick provides critically important warnings and information you need to know before you begin your journey. He also explains how to test the energy and activate and expand it to maximize the psychic potentials of your experience.

Tape 3: MEDITATION—FOCUSING THE VORTEX ENERGY FOR PHYSICAL HEALING—Go to one of the vortex areas and use the tape to go into a deep meditation—the rest will be taken care of. (Dick's most powerful healing tape!)

Tape 4: MEDITATION—FOCUSING CRYSTAL ENERGY IN THE VORTEX—Take a crystal with you into the vortex and use this altered-state tape to expand the energy.

Tape 5: MEDITATION—CALLING IN THE VORTEX SPIRITS—Use in the vortex to open the door to the other side and the spirits that remain there.

Tape 6: MEDITATION—TESTING UNSEEN ENERGY—An altered-state test to check the positive/negative aspects of energy in the vortex, Indian spiritual areas, caves, etc.

Tape 7: PAST-LIFE THERAPY MEDITATION—Combine your energy with that of the vortex and experience the ultimate past-life regression.

Tape 8: THE LEMURIA/SEDONA CONNECTION MEDITATION—Use any of the various methods to explore this fascinating past-present connection.

ASTRAL PROJECTION HYPNOSIS ALBUM

By Dick Sutphen
2 Cassette Tapes (4 Programs)
And a Complete Instruction Book
In a Vinyl Album
$24.95 (Item No. C814)

Hypnosis is the ultimate technique to expand and alter consciousness, so it is the ideal methodology to explore the astral realms. Another conclusion is that different people respond to different techniques and experience the results in different ways. Thus the album is made up of an introduction/preparation tape, followed by a controlled lift-out experiment and two lift-out techniques tapes.

Tape 1A: INTRODUCTION AND PREPARATION—Necessary understanding before you begin your astral projection work. Dick conducts an exercise to ensure successful results. He then goes into the various blocks people may experience when attempting to project and offers some unique techniques to rise above them.

Tape 1B: STANDARD LIFT-OUT—A highly refined version of the hypnotic technique that has proven to be the most successful for the largest number of people. It is this exercise that has convinced many that they have actually projected, for Dick will have participants project outside the seminar room to the parking lot and make notes. When they are awakened, he sends them out to check their accuracy.

Tape 2A: SOUND ACCOMPANIED LIFT-OUT—Dick directs you to relax and allow the electronic sound to deepen your trance. You are instructed to project to any place in the world you desire. At the end of the tape you are called back and awakened with the suggestion to feel relaxed and calm... and to remember everything that transpired.

Tape 2B: VIBRATIONAL LIFT-OUT—Deep hypnosis induction, then you are directed to bring up your vibrations and lift out.

VIEWING PAST LIVES:
The Ascension Technique
By Dick Sutphen (Item No. C833) $39.95
4 Cassette Tapes (8 Programs) & Instruction Book

A unique meditation technique of past-life regression that always works, this album uses a gentle meditative body relaxation, followed by "Ascension Technique" instructions. You don't regress; you go directly back to the past life. You'll experience your past lives before your inner eyes, and the sessions in this album offer a wide new range of explorations.

Tape 1: SPECIAL INSTRUCTIONS—Dick explains how the regressions work and provides information to assure successful results.

Tape 2: GENERAL PAST-LIFE REGRESSION—Each time you use it, you are instructed to back go back to a different lifetime, unless you want to insert overriding instructions and experience a specific past life. Dick will direct you through important aspects of the lifetime—year, place, career, relationships, events, etc., and then, without pain or emotion, you will oberve how you experienced death and your crossover into spirit.

Tape 3: PRE-BIRTH DECISIONS ABOUT YOUR CURRENT LIFE—You are directed back to a time in spirit, on the other side, before you were born into your present life, when you made decisions about your rebirth. Find out why you chose your particular parents, your astrological path and much more.

Tape 4: PAST-LIFE KARMA—What patterns continue to come up for you, lifetime after lifetime, due to a karmic or soul trait? Relationship or health problems? Interest in art, music? Fears, phobias? Wealth, poverty? Through awareness, you can rise above undesirable patterns and become accomplished in talented areas.

Tape 5: PAST-LIFE EXPLORATION WITH A PERSON OF YOUR CHOICE—Find out if you have a past-life tie with your mate, lover, child, new friend, whoever. Dick tells you how to "lock in" on that person in regression. Learn about your relationship today and in the future as joint karma unfolds, and how to rise above any negative aspects.

Tape 6: PAST-LIFE EXPLORATION TO A TIME OR CIVILIZATION OF YOUR CHOICE—Have you always been interested in Egypt? The Civil War? Atlantis? Find out if you ever lived in a particular civilizaton and how this affinity or aversion affects your present "soul awareness."

Tape 7: PAST-LIFE KARMA AFFECTING YOUR PRESENT LIFE—Maybe it is positive: a talent or ability, personality trait or beautiful relationship. Maybe it's negative: health or monetary problems, relationship conflicts, fears or phobias. Wisdom erases karma and the first step is awareness.

Tape 8: INTENSIFYING DEJA VU POTENTIAL—This tape programs you to experience a physical/mental reaction whenever you touch on the subject or timing of one of your past lives. This could be while reading a book, watching TV or a movie, or visiting a new environment. If you've experienced a past life that relates, you'll sense an internal alarm that will make you aware.

PSYCHIC POWERS PROGRAMMING
By Dick Sutphen (Item C832) $32.95
2 Cassette Tapes (4 Programs) Plus 235-Page Book
& Instruction Book

This fantastic album includes a 235-page book: "How to Read the Aura, Practice Psychometry, Telepathy and Clairvoyance" by W. E. Butler, explaining step-by-step exactly what you need to know to develop the ability to use these awareness-expanding parapsychology techniques. The author, W. E. Butler, renowned British parapsychologist, details the four psychic powers that lie within each of us and teaches you how to develop them.

On the cassette tapes, Dick uses his most effective techniques to program you to open and develop in each of the four areas. Each tape can be used either as hypnosis or sleep programming.

Tape 1: AURA READING—Perceive aura emanations that surround every human being and learn to understand their meanings, thus enhancing your awareness of others.

Tape 2: DEVELOPING THE ABILITY OF PSYCHOMETRY—Hold an object in your hand and psychically "know" about the owner or the history of the object.

Tape 3: DEVELOPING TELEPATHIC ABILITY—Telepathy means "feeling at a distance" or "thought transference." Learn to transfer your thoughts, consciousness and will to anyone or any place on earth. Mentally "be there" and perceive what is happening.

Tape 4: DEVELOPING CLAIRVOYANCE—Genuine clairvoyance is a spiritual faculty meaning "clear seeing." It includes the ability to "see" the past, present and future. Dick programs you to open spiritually and make contact with "highly evolved and loving entities of the light" to assist you.

Note: We believe that everyone has the internal power to develop these abilities. Dick has often proven this in his seminars. Yet we want to point out that it takes time and effort. If you want to become a tennis player, you know you're going to have to learn the ground rules and then spend time practicing. If you do, you can become at least a fairly good tennis player. The same is true of the psychic powers described above. If you're willing to read the books, perform the exercises regularly and do your tape programming daily, **YOU WILL DEVELOP YOUR SIXTH SENSE!** It may take a few weeks or few months, but you'll be amazed at what you can do.

SPIRITUAL POWER AFFIRMATIONS
By Dick Sutphen (Item No. C827) $29.95
2 Cassette Tapes (4 Programs) & Instruction Book In a Vinyl Album

Call up the Power! Manifest your deisres! Channel the reality that is yours by divine birthright! The unbelievable power of repeatedly perceiving a positive affirmation is well-documented in metaphysical literature and mind research.

The subconscious mind acts only according to programming and always assists in manifesting that which it accepts as reality. Programming is simply the input it receives in the form of thoughts and experiences. If your subconscious hears something over and over and over again, it will tend to accept the concept. We believe the subconscious taps into the Superconscious and Universal levels of mind to assist you to achieve your divine potential and fulfill your destiny.

In the background is beautiful New Age music. Dick directs a gentle body relaxation and recites the "I Beseech Thee" incantation. Then he repeatedly recites 10 Spiritual Power Affirmations. Each tape is a on a different subject. Over and over, these powerful affirmations are communicated to every level of your body and mind. If you speak the affirmations along with Dick, they will be all the more powerful. If you use the tape as it comes, you'll experience the programming in a meditative, altered state of consciousness. You may also use them as sleep programming, for the ending is structured so you may choose to awaken or drift off into a natural sleep. If you'd like to use the tapes while driving or any other activity, simply run the tape forward past the initial "body relaxation." Each side runs approximately 20 minutes.

Tape 1: ABUNDANCE—I live in a Universe of abundance and I now rise above my limited awareness to claim my share of my divine legacy. ■ I channel abundance for the greater good in harmony with Universal Law. ■ From the limitless Universal supply, I now attract success as a reflection of the abundance of All That Is.

Tape 2: HEALTH & HEALING—I thankfully accept the divine healing of my body and my radiant health reflects Universal Love. ■ I channel the unlimited power of divine light through every cell of my body and mind. ■ I now choose to experience joy and vitality as a reflection of the omnipresence of All That Is.

Tape 3: PEACE, BALANCE & HARMONY—Regardless of external circumstances, peace, balance and harmony are mine by simply viewing my life from a perspective of unconditional love. ■ I now choose to experience my life as divine tranquility and thus experience my birthright.

Tape 4: SELF-REALIZATION—From this moment on, I radiate self-realization for I now acccept this godly awareness as my birthright. ■ My desires are clear and I channel the power to make them manifest ... I ask it ... I beseech it, and mark it ... AND SO IT IS.

KNOW THY HIGHER SELF
By Dick Sutphen (Item No. RA201) $45.00
4 Cassette Tapes (8 Programs) In a Vinyl Album

The basic Reincarnationists course and an intensive seminar on reincarnation and karma, this album is an explanation of metaphysics from a Reincarnationist's viewpoint. Founded as a nonprofit organization in 1984 by Dick Sutphen, Reincarnationists is a philosophy/religion of self that you don't join, you live!

Based on 18 years' experience in regressing over 55,000 people into their past lives, Dick relates how it appears to work and much new information you won't find in any of his best-selling books ... or anywhere else!

If you sincerely want to end suffering, evolve spiritually and rise above your karma, the wisdom on these tapes can change your life!

Tape 1: THE SUPREME UNIVERSAL LAW—KARMA I—Even if you thiink you really understand karma, this newly channeled information is sure to expand your awareness and generate a great deal of self-processing.

Tape 2: WHAT IS, IS—KARMA II—Coverage of the three general areas of karma: Self-Testing, Reward, and Self-Punishment, and the five basic karma categories: Balancing, Physical, False Fear, False Guilt, and Developed Ability/Awareness, plus the awareness to end suffering (everything in your life that causes mental discomfort).

Tape 3: THE 7 KARMIC PATHS, 7 DHARMIC DIRECTIONS & 7 SOUL GOALS—You are currently walking one of 7 Karmic Paths (which you are capable of changing), and you were born with one of 7 Soul Goals and one of 7 Dharmic Directions (man's duty to self and to society). Are you on purpose? If you don't know, you certainly need to find out.

Tape 4: REINCARNATION—THE WAY IT REALLY WORKS—Dick's controversial explanation isn't the one you expect, but it clears up the inconsistencies you've wondered about. He covers your oversoul and lineage, parallel incarnations and walk-ins.

Tape 5: VIBRATIONAL RATES & ASTRAL LEVELS—You were born with a vibrational rate earned from past programming and past lives. Are you raising or lowering it by the way you live your life? (You may be surprised!) Also explains the 7 Astral Levels.

Tape 6: THE 15 REINCARNATIONISTS TENETS TO END SUFFERING & EVOLVE SPIRITUALLY: THE MOST IMPORTANT UNIVERSAL LAWS; MEDITATION INSTRUCTIONS—Awareness to immediately change your life. It' that simple! (Although not that easy!)

Tape 7: REINCARNATIONISTS MEDITATION SESSION WITH OPEN CENTER, so you can begin to find your own answers.

Tape 8: ATTRACTING A MASTER MEDITATION—A powerful, directed meditation to make contact with your spiritual Master/teacher and attain spiritually evolving awareness.

HOW TO RAPIDLY DEVELOP PSYCHIC ABILITY
By Dick Sutphen (Item No. C837) $24.95
2 Tapes (4 Programs) & Instruction Book

Everyone has a psychic sixth sense they can develop if they know how and are willing to program and practice! If you seriously want to be psychic, this two-tape album will open the door to an entirely new reality.

Tape 1: THE 10 PRIMARY EXERCISES TO DEVELOP PSYCHIC ABILITY—This is a talk and workshop in which Dick covers psychic reception techniques, how to recognize psychic input while fully conscious and he relates the 10 most effective ways to develop your psychic powers. These are techniques you will begin to use on a daily basis.

Tape 2: EXPANSION OF PSYCHIC ABILITIES HYPNOSIS—After a safe, hypnotic induction (from which you are given a self-release technique) your guides and Masters are called in, and you are instructed to open your mind to your psychic abilities. When the programming suggestions are completed, you are instructed to ask any questions you would like to have answered. Next, trust the impressions or thoughts that come into your mind as an answer. You'll discover a very high degree of accuracy that will increase the more you use the tape, which also programs your general development of psychic abilities. Your subconscious mind will always manipulate circumstances of your outer reality to align with your inner programming. Thus, when you are hypnotically programmed to become psychic, it works if you use your tapes every day.

Tape 3: SUBLIMINAL PSYCHIC ABILITIES PROGRAMMING—Use as background music while you drive, work or play. The powerful phrases are hidden behind beautiful relaxing music. You consciously hear only the music while your subconscious mind hears and acts on the suggestions. The Suggestions: The psychic power you desire is within you and is your divine right. ■ Infinite spirit gives you the wisdom to increase your psychic powers. You trust the intuitive process. ■ You have extrasensory and precognitive abilities. ■ You now open these channels so the powers of your mind work for you. ■ You follow the magical path of intuition and your psychic powers increase tenfold. ■ Every day you become more and more psychic.

Tape 4: SUBLIMINAL PROGRAMMING WITH BODY RELAXATION—This is the same music and suggestions as on Tape 3, but at the beginning of the tape Dick also directs a body relaxation for your conscious mind over the music and is then quiet until the end of the tape, when he instructs you to awaken or drift off into a natural sleep if you desire.

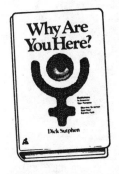

WHY ARE YOU HERE?
By Dick Sutphen (Item No. C836) $29.95
2 Cassette Tapes (4 Programs) & Instruction Book In a Vinyl Album

Meditations to discover your purpose: Dharmic Direction, Soul Goal and Karmic Path.

If your life isn't working, it may be because you don't really know why you are here, living in these turbulent times on the earth plane of existence. This album can change that. It can provide you with the direction to create a brand-new reality .By discovering your true purpose, you can attain mental and spiritual fulfillment.

Tape 1A: DHARMIC DIRECTION MEDITATION—You were born with a "dharmic direction" and a "soul goal." In other words, you have a purpose or mission to accomplish during your lifetime ... it is the reason you are here! According to classic metaphysics, dharma is man's duty to himself and society. Through your karma, your experiences create the "character" required to carry out your dharma ... your destiny. There are seven general dharmic directions and your purpose is to explore one of these paths in conjunction with a particular soul goal that you chose prior to your birth. In an altered-state-of-consciousness session, Dick will direct you to discover, for yourself, your dharmic direction and to seek Higher guidance in regard to fulfilling your destiny.

Tape 1B: SOUL GOAL MEDITATION—In addition to having chosen one of seven dharmic directions prior to your birth, you also chose one of seven basic soul goals. You can have more than one goal, but one will be most important. Everyone has definite karmic life priorities. While you are in an altered state, Dick will direct you to discover your soul goals and the order of your priorities.

Tape 2A: KARMIC PATH MEDITATION—There are seven basic karmic paths—seven routes to fulfilling your destiny once you are clear as to your purpose. This beautiful guided session will assist you to make conscious decisions which will surely not only change your current life, but maybe the direction of your future lifetimes as well.

Tape 2B: "WHY AREN'T I HAPPY AND FULFILLED?" MEDITATION—This session uses several techniques including human-potential processing and past-life regression to uncover hidden blocks that are keeping you from enjoying the life you know is possible. Just one new bit of awareness as a result of this session could change your life.

SOULMATES

By Dick Sutphen (Item No. C835) $29.95
2 Cassette Tapes (4 Programs) & Instruction Book

If you want to really do something to bring about the meeting with your soulmate, this album uses the most powerful techniques in existence to assist you to create your desired reality. It appears that there are three kinds of soulmates: ☐ **Karmic Soulmate:** Someone you are drawn to, to learn important unlearned lessons from the past. This may be a temporary relationship. ☐ **Companion Soulmate:** Someone with whom you are destined to share love and the accomplishment of a project or specific mission. This may not be a lifelong relationship. ☐ **Twin Soul:** A perfect partner for you. You share the same vibrational level and a lineage of past lives. Usually a lifelong relationship which will allow you both to more easily fulfill your "dharmic directions" and accomplish your "soul goals."

Tape 1A: FINDING YOUR SOULMATE—A Higher-Self Deep-Level Meditation Session in which you are directed to create the space to meet your soulmate. This involves questions which you must be clear about before this can transpire. You are then guided to superconsciously explore potentials to manifest the meeting with your soulmate and the bonding that will follow.

Tape 1B: SOULMATE VERIFICATION—A deep meditation session designed to check out an individual you feel might be a soulmate. You'll perceive previous lifetimes you shared plus an overview of your karmic relationship. You'll explore the proper action to take in regard to the relationship.

Tapes 2A & 2B: SUBLIMINAL SOULMATE PROGRAMMING—Suggestions are hidden behind beautiful New-Age music. You consciously hear only the relaxing music while your subconscious mind hears the suggestions and acts to assist you to bring them into reality. **The Suggestions:** ■ You now create the space to meet your soulmate. ■ You are now open and ready for a twin-soul relationship. ■ You call down the Power of Powers and draw your soulmate to you. ■ An expanding spiritual light within prepares you for your unconditional love. ■ All your relationship desires now become manifest.

HIGHER-SELF EXPLORATIONS

By Dick Sutphen
2 Cassette Tapes (4 Programs)
And a Complete Instruction Book
In a Vinyl Album
$24.95 (Item No. C811)

Explore areas previously beyond the reach of the material world. Dick opens channels that will support your consciousness expansion. All hypnosis inductions on this album are "up, up, higher, higher," instead of "down, down, deeper, deeper." Suggestions for white light and self-release are given.

Tape 1: TRANSCENDENCE: ACHIEVING THE ULTIMATE LEVEL—A beautiful tape produced with music. It offers the ultimate induction for transcending the physical and entering the mental, Higher-Self realms. Contact is established with Guides or Masters.

Tape 2: VERBAL CHANNELING—Establish contact with a highly-evolved and friendly entity and channel their wisdom through your vocal cords. Time is allowed for the channeling experience.

Tape 3: DIRECT WRITING—The tape provides protection, then induces an ultra-expansion of consciousness. Dick directs you to place your fingers on the typewriter keys or hold a pen to paper, and to be open to receiving what comes through from a highly evolved and friendly entity, or from another aspect of your own consciousness.

Tape 4: TELEPATHIC CONTACT ON A SUPERCONSCIOUS LEVEL—Tap in on the superconscious of others now living on Earth, and communicate directly through thought-to-thought transmission. Those who believe in and develop this ability will find it extremely effective.

NOTE: The tapes in this album are for well-conditioned subjects. If you are not hypnosis-conditioned, plan to use Tape 1 once a day for four weeks prior to using the other three programs.

THE PAST-LIFE HYPNOTIC REGRESSION COURSE

By Dick Sutphen (Item No. C801) $29.95
2 Cassette Tapes (4 Programs)/Regression Manual

This is our best-selling album. It has been used safely and successfully by thousands of people over the years to discover and explore their own past lives. The album includes a lengthy Instruction Manual which, when used with the tapes, ensures effective results. This course is carefully structured to properly condition you, step by step. If the instructions are followed, anyone will be able to draw upon subconscious memories of other lives. Most people will perceive numerous past lives by continuing to use the tapes. You can also use them to bring forth more and more details about any incarnation you desire to explore in more depth. There is nothing mystical about the process. We all have the ability to expand our awareness of the true nature of reality.

Tape 1: PAST-LIFE CONDITIONING—You are hypnotized and carefully conditioned to perceive past-life memories from your own subconscious mind. This is accomplished with strong suggestions: "In the memory banks of your subconscious mind there is a memory of everything that has ever happened to you: every thought, every action, ever deed...from this life you are now living or from any of your past lives!"

Tape 2: PAST-LIFE REGRESSION TAPE—In deep hypnosis your subconscious mind is instructed to choose a lifetime that would be of value for you to explore at this time. You will be instructed to re-experience only positive happenings and occurences from that life, which you will witness as an observer without pain or emotion. You'll move through a tunnel to your past life and will then be guided through several different important positive events. Dick uses "no-fail" techniques to establish your name, the year and country you lived in.

Tape 3: PAST-LIFE INVOLVEMENT WITH YOUR PRESENT MATE OR LOVER—or any one else you'd like to know about. After the induction, you are instructed to think about the person in your current life that you would like to know about. The tape takes you back into your past to see if, indeed, you have shared a previous incarnation and if so, how it relates to your present relationship.

Tape 4: SELF-HYPNOSIS WITH OPEN CENTER—This tape is included for other hypnotic programming and exploratory uses. There is a quiet time of several minutes between the induction and awakening at which you are directed to "think-in" your own suggestions. You can program yourself to accomplish goals, overcome problems or develop new abilities with this tape if you use it creatively.

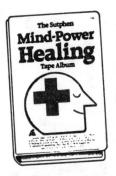

THE SUTPHEN MIND-POWER HEALING TAPE ALBUM

(Item No. C830) $24.95
2 Cassette Tapes (4 Programs) & Instruction Book

Like a first-aid kit, this is an album you'll want to have around for use when you, or someone close to you, needs to use it. Research has proven that your mind has the power to assist you to heal. By combining hypnosis, sleep programming and subliminal programming, you maximize the positive, healing input to your subconscious mind. This album is not intended as a replacement for standard medical aid; it is to assist it.

Tape 1: PSYCHIC HEALING HYPNOSIS—In hypnosis, Dick instructs you to communicate with your body and call in your guides and the spiritual forces to help create healing. Positive affirmations are used for a strong, healthy body, and post-hypnotic suggestions are given for continued acceleration of the healing process.

Tape 2: HEALING ACCELERATION HYPNOSIS—Structured to speed up the natural body-healing process with strong suggestions and cybernetic affirmation techniques. Recovery time can be accelerated with positive mental input. Use on colds, the flu, after surgery...or even on chronic and degenerative diseases.

Tape 3: HEALING ACCELERATION SLEEP PROGRAMMING—Simply listen to this tape as you fall asleep at night. Supports the suggestions on the tape above to accelerate recovery time; promotes healthy dream programming.

Tape 4: SUBLIMINAL HEALING ACCELERATION PROGRAMMING—Listen to this tape at least once a day while going about your normal activities or even while driving in your car. It is relaxing, mellow music, but behind the music is a programming voice feeding suggestions to your subconscious mind. You won't hear the voice consciously, but it is there and it's very effective.

The Subliminal Suggestions: You are surrounded by a divine blue healing light. ■ Divine light streams through your cells, healing you quickly and completely. ■ You have the power and ability to accelerate your healing. ■ Your body is filled with positive, healing energy and you accelerate the healing. ■ Your mind is all-powerful and you now use it rapidly to heal yourself. ■ You now heal yourself...you now heal yourself...you now heal yourself. ■ Each minute...each hour, you move more rapidly toward total healing. ■ You are healing...you are healed. ■ You accept total health as your reality...and it now becomes your reality. ■ You now focus the healing power of the universe upon your body and mind.

THE METAPHYSICAL AWARENESS HYPNOSIS ALBUM

By Dick Sutphen (Item No. C825) $29.95
2 Cassette Tapes (4 Programs) & Instruction Book

No matter what your background in metaphysics, these sessions are sure to expand your awareness, allowing you and those close to you to explore the reality of generally accepted metaphysical concepts.

Tape 1: PRE-BIRTH PLANNING SESSION—A HYPNOTIC REGRESSION: You are directed back to a time prior to being born into your current life—to a time in spirit that you made decisions about the life journey you were about to embark upon. You have a reason for being here; you have a primary purpose or mission to accomplish in experiencing your current life. To become fully aware of that purpose or mission may assist you in fulfilling your life plan, and it may help you to attain a unique sense of peace and balance.

Tape 2: THREE SPECIAL LIVES—HYPNOTIC REGRESSION SESSION: In the memory banks of your subconscious mind there is a memory of everything that has ever happened to you, including memories of all your past lives. First you are regressed back to your most psychic lifetime and asked questions about the life you lived. Next, you are directed to the lifetime in which you express more natural talent than in any other. The third is a great lifetime. There is one lifetime in which you achieved a position of importance, far beyond any other of your incarnations and you will explore it once again.

Tape 3: MEETING YOUR GUIDE AND MASTERS—HYPNOSIS SESSION: Your primary guide has been with you since birth and will remain with you throughout your life, always doing all within his or her power to assist you in accomplishing your mission or fulfilling your purpose. Those intuitive feelings about what you should or shouldn't do are often being sent to you by your guide. Masters are the wise souls who often assist you in special learning. This session is carefully structured for you to meet and interact, first with your guide and then with any Masters working with you.

Tape 4: AN ASTRAL PLANES TOUR—HYPNOSIS SESSION: On a Superconscious level you are fully aware of time spent on the other side between lifetimes, and of the vibrational levels you evolve up through as you evolve spiritually. You are no stranger to the astral world; it is your true home. For now, for awhile, you are here using a physical body to experience the manifest world and the potentials for spiritual growth that are offered on the physical plane. Your guide and Masters are called in to assist you on your journey to the levels of the upper astral plane.

PAST-LIFE THERAPY REGRESSION TAPE ALBUM

By Dick Sutphen (Item No. AX901) $29.95
2 Cassette Tapes (4 Programs) & Instruction Book

Past-life Therapy has become widely recognized as an extremely valuable technique to eliminate problems. All of your feelings, hang-ups, fears and phobias come from some definite event or series of events in your past. It is our experience that the past includes prior incarnations. Even marriage and sexual problems often relate to previous lives.

If you have a problem or if you're not as happy or successful as you want to be, there is subconscious programming that must be overcome. Your conscious and subconscious minds are in conflict—consciously you want something, yet you continue to retain the problem subconsciously, creating mediocrity or failure.

We offer you four past-life sessions and a complete manual—you can use the sessions over and over again to explore for yourself, your family or friends the past lives that are causing present-day difficulties.

Tape 1: BACK-TO-THE-CAUSE REGRESSION—This is structured for you to decide what you desire to investigate (e.g., a fear, talent, relationship, affliction, unusual situation). You are directed to focus upon it as you are guided back in time to the origin of the situation in your past—your current life or a past life. You are instructed to perceive the cause without pain or emotion, only as an observer. You are awakened with the strong suggestion to release the past if it is negative.

Tape 2: WISDOM ERASES KARMA—Once you know the cause, this expanded-state-of-consciousness session guides you into your Higher-Self to achieve a karmic overview of the situation so you can fully understand the fear behind the problem and what you need to accept to completely eliminate negativity from your life once and for all.

Tape 3: OVERSOUL AWARENESS OF YOUR LIFE PLAN—A Higher-Self expanded-state-of-consciousness session to explore your life from a multi-life perspective. The session goal is to explore your primary purpose and present level of awareness. You will become aware how you can accelerate the evolutive process.

Tape 4: PAST-LIFE TALENTS AND ABILITIES—A multi-life regression to seek out forgotten valuable knowledge from your former lives. This session has launched many people on new careers or opened the door to latent abilities. If you developed a particular talent or ability in your past, it should be exceptionally natural and easy to do it again.

MAKE CHECKS PAYABLE TO
Valley of the Sun Publishing
Box 3004, Agoura Hills, CA 91301
818/889-1575

ORDER FORM
S1

Name

Address

City   **State**   **Zip**

Item Number	Name of Item	Qty.	Price

NO CASH OR C.O.D.'s PLEASE

Prices subject to change without notice. Offers in other Valley of the Sun catalogs do not relate to any items offered here. VISA and MasterCard orders, please call collect: 1-800-421-6603.

CANADIAN—Please include $7.50 extra in U.S. funds.
FOREIGN—Please write for a PRO FORMA invoice.

MERCHANDISE TOTAL	
CA SALES TAX (Residents only. 6%)	
SHIPPING CHARGE	$2.50
ORDER TOTAL	

MAKE CHECKS PAYABLE TO
Valley of the Sun Publishing
Box 3004, Agoura Hills, CA 91301
818/889-1575

ORDER FORM
S1

Name

Address

City   **State**   **Zip**

Item Number	Name of Item	Qty.	Price

NO CASH OR C.O.D.'s PLEASE

Prices subject to change without notice. Offers in other Valley of the Sun catalogs do not relate to any items offered here. VISA and MasterCard orders, please call collect: 1-800-421-6603.

CANADIAN—Please include $7.50 extra in U.S. funds.
FOREIGN—Please write for a PRO FORMA invoice.

MERCHANDISE TOTAL	
CA SALES TAX (Residents only. 6%)	
SHIPPING CHARGE	$2.50
ORDER TOTAL	